CROATIA:
MYTH AND REALITY

CIS Monographs

Arcadia, California

1992

Printed in the United States of America by

CIS Monographs

Croatian Information Service
Post Office Box 3025
Arcadia, CA 91006 USA

Order Additional Copies from
CIS Monographs
Post Office Box 661894
Sacramento, CA 95866-1894 USA

COPYRIGHT © 1992 BY THE AUTHOR

ISBN 0-9633625-1-8

Petar Radielović
Editor

This monograph is respectfully dedicated to Professor George J. Prpić.

The author gratefully acknowledges the contributions and support of his many friends in the Croatian community.

CONTENTS

INTRODUCTION

CROATIA AND THE CROATIANS

MYTH: "THE CROATIANS ASKED TO JOIN YUGOSLAVIA"

MYTH: "A CROATIAN USTAŠE TERRORIST ASSASSINATED KING ALEXANDER"

MYTH: "ALL CROATIANS WERE FASCISTS DURING WORLD WAR II; ALL SERBS WERE PRO-ALLIED"

MYTH: "THE BASKET OF HUMAN EYEBALLS"

MYTH: "TWO MILLION SERBS DIED"

MYTH: "THE CROATIANS EXECUTED DOZENS OF AMERICAN AIRMEN"

MYTH: "THERE WAS NO RETRIBUTION AGAINST THE CROATIANS AFTER WORLD WAR II"

MYTH: "BORDERS WERE DRAWN TO BENEFIT CROATIA"

MYTH: "SERBS HAVE NO RIGHTS IN CROATIA"

MYTH: "TUDJMAN IS A RECENT CONVERT FROM COMMUNISM TO DEMOCRACY"

MYTH: "THE CROATIAN COAT OF ARMS IS A FASCIST SYMBOL"

THE FINAL MYTH: "YUGOSLAVIA"

BIBLIOGRAPHY

INTRODUCTION

It is often said that truth is the first casualty in war. In June of 1991 war broke out in Europe for the first time since World War II as Serbia attacked Slovenia and Croatia. At the same time another war, a war of propaganda and mythology, was launched in the world press. Identical stories surfaced with identical words in different publications written by different journalists throughout the world. The attack was two-pronged. One goal was to tar the fledgling Croatian government with the brush of Fascism, despite the fact that the President of Croatia was a Partisan war hero who fought against the Fascists during World War II.

Another purpose was to mask the reasons for Serbian aggression and to blur the realities of a war prosecuted solely to gain territory and to maintain centralized Communism in what was Yugoslavia. At first the disinformation was limited to the writings of avowed leftists such as Alexander Cockburn and Serbian apologists like Congresswoman Helen Delich Bentley, David Martin, and Nora Beloff. As the war dragged on from weeks to months, the words and phrases of Serbian mythology appeared over and over again in an ever widening circle that would eventually include the editorial pages of such highly respected journals as the *Christian Science Monitor* and *New York Times*. Yet few of the charges and allegations of the campaign were new. The history of Serbian disinformation can be traced back to the origins of Yugoslavia in 1918. The Communist Party controlled *Tanjug* news agency and Television Belgrade continued the battle that was lost in the diplomatic community as one nation after another recognized a free and independent Croatia.

On November 20, 1991 headlines around the world screamed "Croatian Militias Slit Throats of 41 Children." Reuters news agency reported: "The children, between 5 and 7 years old, reportedly were found with their throats cut in the cellar of the kindergarten in Borovo Naselje after Croatian forces abandoned it during the weekend." The children were, according to the report, all Serbs.

This story demonstrates mythology in the making. It was carried on every electronic network and in newspapers throughout the world without any form of confirmation. That the village in question had been under siege for months, that all children had been evacuated months before, and that obviously no kindergarten classes had been held anywhere in the war zone for some time did not seem to catch the attention of a single editor. The following day some papers ran the Reuters retraction in small print after the twenty-two year-old Serbian photographer, Goran Mikić, admitted that he had fabricated the story. In Belgrade the press never printed the retraction and in fact later cited the non-incident in its news coverage as a part of its propaganda campaign against Croatia.

Propaganda is defined as information and opinions, especially prejudiced ones, spread to influence people in favor of or against some doctrine or idea. Myth is defined as an old traditional story or legend. Mythology represents a body of myths. Over the past seventy years a great deal of propaganda has become mythology with a life of its own, growing and changing with each retelling. Myths were not only resurrected and embellished by propagandists, but by well-intended journalists and others attempting to understand and to justify the Serbian wars of aggression. Regardless of the motivation of those who repeat the myths, the result is always the same. Another generation is introduced to the mythology created to keep the Croatian nation in bondage.

Some myths are new, others are very old. The myth of the forty-one children reported on one day and retracted the next will no doubt find its way into some history book, somewhere, as fact. It will become a part of the negative mythology or "black legend" that casts its shadow on the Croatian nation.

On the following pages both the established myths and emerging myths will be explored and exposed to reality. Some have simple explanations, others are more complex. Some are gruesome and distasteful. This monograph is intended to shed light, not heat and to bring the myths from the shadows into the realm of reality.

CROATIA AND THE CROATIANS

Croatia emerged as a unified nation state in 925 AD and, through a personal union under a single king, joined what would become the Austro-Hungarian Empire in the twelfth century. Throughout the history of the Empire, Croatia maintained varying degrees of autonomy with its own *Ban* or Viceroy and *Sabor* or Parliament which first met in 1533. Following World War I, Croatia was absorbed into the new artificial state that would become Yugoslavia. The first Yugoslavia, from 1918-1941 was little more than an extension of Serbia with a Serbian king, ruling from the Serbian capital of Belgrade with Serbian laws. This marked the first time in history that the Serbs, Croats, Slovenes, Montenegrins and Macedonians had lived together in a single state. The history of royalist Yugoslavia was marked by the brutal suppression of Croatian political, human and civil rights. The Croatian nation rallied around the Croatian Peasant Party and Stjepan Radić, its elderly, nearly blind, pacifist leader. Radić, along with four other Croatian leaders, was gunned down by a Serbian Deputy on the floor of Parliament in 1928. King Alexander Karageorgević followed this blow by declaring himself absolute dictator and banning all political parties. Croatian Parliamentary Deputy Ante Pavelić then formed the *Ustaše* or "Rebel" Croatian Liberation Movement to gain Croatian independence by force. Alexander was assassinated in 1934 and was succeeded by his cousin Prince Regent Paul, an Oxford educated half-Russian who cared little about politics or Yugoslavia.

World War II

Between 1934 and 1941 Yugoslavia moved closer and closer to Hitler under the leadership of Milan Stojadinović who formed his own "Green Shirts" and adopted the title *Vodja* or *Führer*. Later Premier Dragiša Cvetković would lead Yugoslavia into the Axis fold with Mussolini and Hitler on March 24, 1941. Almost immediately a military *coup* was staged by two Serbian air force generals assisted by the British Special Operations Executive.

Finding instability on his southern flank unacceptable on the eve of the invasion of the Soviet Union, Hitler ordered the immediate conquest of Yugoslavia. The Serbian-dominated army surrendered without a fight. The Government and Serbian royal family fled to Britain with millions in gold and established the Yugoslav Government-in-Exile which laid the entire blame for the war and defeat on the Croatians.

Pavelić's *Ustaše*, with its large underground network, immediately took control of Croatia including Bosnia and Hercegovina. The new Croatian state was divided into German and Italian occupation zones while Italy annexed large parts of Dalmatian Croatia outright. Croatia joined the Axis, sent troops to the Eastern Front and enacted anti-Semitic and anti-Serbian legislation. S e r b i a became a Nazi puppet state under General Milan Nedić who continued the persecution of Jews, Gypsies and Croatians that had begun under the royalist regime before the War. Tens of thousands perished in the multi-faceted war among Communist Partisans, German, Italian, Croatian, Serbian, and even Russian Cossack forces. In the end, it would be the Communist-backed Partisan army led by a Croatian, Marshal Josip Broz Tito, with the backing of the Red Army which would emerge victorious.

The Second Yugoslavia

After World War II, Yugoslavia was reconstituted as a Communist federal republic with the promise of equality for all of its nations and peoples. As in most Communist states, promises were not fulfilled. A ruthless secret police compounded by the economic and political exploitation of Croatia led hundreds of thousands of young Croatians to seek freedom and prosperity abroad. After the purge of secret police chief Aleksander Ranković in 1966, a new air of freedom developed in Croatia known as "The Croatian Spring." Less known in the West than the "Prague Spring," this great liberalization was crushed by the Communists in late 1971. One of the first victims of the new repression was a dissident former Partisan war hero and Yugoslav Army general, Franjo Tudjman. The events of 1971 put into motion events twenty years later that would result in Croatian independence.

The death of Tito in 1980 led to increased demands for democracy and a market-based economy as well as for greater autonomy by Croatia and Slovenia from the Serbian-controlled central government. As Western-oriented Slovenia and Croatia moved quickly toward democratic reform, Eastern-oriented Serbia struggled to maintain Communist authoritarianism and a centralized government. In 1990 Dr. Franjo Tudjman became the first freely elected President of Croatia in over a half century.

Free and democratic elections in Croatia and Slovenia demonstrated a commitment to the democratic process, the protection of human rights, and the development of a free market economy in those Republics. Croatia immediately began negotiations in mid-1990 toward the formation of a loose confederation of nations that would have granted national autonomy while preserving Yugoslavia in some form.

The Republic of Serbia refused all attempts at negotiation and engaged in massive human rights violations against the Albanian majority in the province of Kosova, dismantling its Parliament and purging its government, media, and educational system of Muslims and non-Communists. The Serbian leader, Slobodan Milošević, remained committed to a single party, totalitarian regime in Serbia and throughout Yugoslavia.

Spurred on by Milošević, Serbs in Croatia launched a well-planned armed insurrection on August 17, 1990, attacking police stations and blockading the main highway south of the Croatian capital of Zagreb. When Croatian police attempted to stop the violence, the central government dispatched the Serbian-controlled air force and army to "restore order." In 1991, after months of fruitless negotiations and increased violence by the Serbian minority in Croatia, fueled by the Serbian government and military, the Croatians voted for independence. On June 25, 1991, Croatia and Slovenia declared themselves to be free and independent of Serbia and Yugoslavia.

Independence and Aggression

Under the pretense of protecting the Serbian minority in Croatia, a full-scale war was launched against Croatia by the Serbian-Yugoslav armed forces and Serbian militias. Croatia abided by over a dozen cease fires only to see the army regroup and attack again. By the end of 1991, over one-third of Croatia's territory had been seized, the city of Vukovar and others totally destroyed and thousands of Croatians had been killed. In December 1991, the Serbian government openly admitted that it aimed to annex territory in Croatia and Bosnia-Hercegovina in order to form a new "Greater Serbia."

On January 15, 1992 the European Community recognized the independence of Croatia and most of the world's major powers followed suit. Notably, the United

States government headed by George Bush held back on recognition of Croatia and Slovenia until after United Nations peacekeeping forces had been moved into Croatia. Bush's Deputy Secretary of State and chief advisor on what was Yugoslavia was Lawrence Eagleburger whom the press dubbed "Lawrence of Serbia." Eagleburger had close personal and financial ties with the Communist leadership of Serbia as well as Yugoslav banks and arms industries. Despite Eagleburger's friendship with Communist Serbia, even the United States was eventually forced to condemn Serbia's expansionist aggression and recognize Croatia in April of 1992.

On April 26, 1992, Serbia declared the birth of a new Federal Yugoslavia and became the last nation in Europe to remove the red star from its flag. The history of the three Yugoslavias has been filled with mythology, but no myth was greater than the myth that Yugoslavia ever really existed.

MYTH: "THE CROATIANS ASKED TO JOIN YUGOSLAVIA"

Myth: The people of Croatia asked to join Serbia in forming Yugoslavia in 1918.

Reality: The people of Croatia did not ask to join Serbia in 1918. The elected representatives of the Croatian people voted for a "Neutral and Peasant Republic of Croatia" in 1918.

The Yugoslav Committee

The basis of the myth that Croatia willingly joined Serbia in 1918 is to be found in the complex history of the Yugoslav Committee. The Yugoslav Committee was formed by exiles living outside the Croatian homeland during World War I. The Committee was led by Franjo Supilo and Ante Trumbić and included the famous Croatian sculptor Ivan Meštrović. Each repudiated the Committee within a few years of the founding of Yugoslavia.

"Yugoslavs" were Serbian, Croatian and Slovenian people who identified themselves with the movement toward a single Yugoslav or South Slavic state. Exiled Yugoslavs living in North America and Britain were the primary supporters of the Yugoslav Committee. Having established offices in London and Paris as early as 1915, the Yugoslav Committee became an active lobby for the cause of a united South Slav state during the First World War.

The concept of a united South Slavic state had been discussed by Croatian and Slovenian intellectuals since the mid-nineteenth century. However, the "Yugoslav Idea" did not mature from the conceptual to practical state of planning. Few of those promoting such an entity had given any serious consideration to what form the new state should take. Nevertheless, the Yugoslav Committee issued a manifesto calling for the formation of such a South Slavic state on May 12, 1915. The document, like the rhetoric of those who produced it, was vague concerning the form and system of government. It received little official recognition.

At the same time Serbia, led by Nikola Pašić's pan-Serbian Radical Party, saw the "Yugoslav" concept as a useful tool in the long sought development of a "Greater Serbia." As the War dragged on, the Allies began to think of the concept of Yugoslavia as a blocking force in the Balkans to counter future German expansionism. Although no formal agreement was announced until July 1917, the Yugoslav Committee and the Serbian Government-in-Exile worked hand-in-hand from November 1916 onward.

On July 20, 1917 the Serbian government and the Yugoslav Committee issued the text of an agreement known as the Declaration of Corfu which called for the formation of a multi-national state. The document was deliberately mute as to whether the government would take the form of Western-oriented Croatia or of the Eastern-oriented Serbia. The vast majority of the Serbian, Croatian and Slovenian people had no knowledge of the declaration made by a small group of exiled intellectuals and the Serbian Government-in-Exile. Nonetheless, the signers claimed to speak for all South Slavic peoples and the Declaration of Corfu became the justification claimed by Serbia for the forced unification of Croatians and Slovenes under the Serbian crown.

The Kingdom of Serbs, Croats and Slovenes

As the War drew to a close, the Austro-Hungarian Empire began to disintegrate. The Croatian *Sabor* or Parliament met in Zagreb on October 29, 1918 to declare "the Kingdom of Croatia, Slavonia and Dalmatia" to be a free and independent state. The Habsburg Crown recognized Croatia and transferred the Austro-Hungarian fleet to the Croatian government on October 31st. The Croatian government in Zagreb was fully formed before the fall of Austria on November 3, Germany on November 11, and Hungary on November 13. The Yugoslav National Council of Slovenes, Croats and Serbs was organized in Zagreb on October 15, 1918. This twenty-eight member Council was self-appointed, not elected. Although its president was a Slovene, the Council was dominated by Svetozar Pribićević, a Serb. On November 24th this self-appointed group called for a common state with Serbia. This is the body so often cited as having "asked" to join Yugoslavia.

The mythology overlooks another Congress held just blocks away on the very next day. This was the Congress of Stjepan Radić's Croatian Peasant Party attended by almost three thousand elected delegates from every part of Croatia. The Peasant Party was the largest and most popular party in Croatia at that time and would remain so during the period between the Wars. It won absolute majorities in every subsequent election. This Congress assailed the National Council as arbitrary and unconstitutional and unanimously adopted a resolution calling for a "Neutral and Peasant Republic of Croatia." Following this Congress, there were huge demonstrations in the streets of Zagreb supporting independence.

Zagreb's brief jubilation quickly changed to the sober realization that Croatia would again be ruled from a foreign capital as Italian, French and French African forces invaded from the west and Serbian troops invaded from the east.

On December 1, 1918, Serbian Prince Alexander announced the formation of the Kingdom of Serbs, Croats and Slovenes, with a Serbian King ruling from the Serbian capital of Belgrade. Despite the neutral sounding name, the country was called Yugoslavia by the diplomatic community almost from the beginning. Ironically, at the Paris Peace Conference the Yugoslav delegation openly insisted that it be known as the "Serbian Delegation."

The Paris Peace Conference

At the Peace Conference itself, the Croatians submitted a petition to President Wilson calling for an independent Croatia. With over 150,000 signatures and the notation that another 450,000 signatures had been seized by the Serbian Army, the document specifically asked:

> That Mr. Wilson and the representatives of the great Powers should recognize the independence of the Croatian people;
>
> That an international Commission should be sent to Croatia to inquire;
>
> That a Constituent Assembly should be formed so that the Croatian people be free to decide their fate;
>
> That the Serbian Army be withdrawn;
>
> That the *Sabor*, should be respected as being alone authorized to the making of laws in Croatia; to-day, they are being dictated by Serbia and executed in the most brutal manner by the military.

Although submitted to the Paris Peace Conference on May 4th, 1919, the objections of the Croatian people were noted and then ignored by the United States and other so-called "Great Powers." President Wilson's famed *Fourteen Points* for which America had fought a World War were undergoing a metamorphosis at the Conference. Point X originally called for "...the freest opportunity of autonomous development" for the nations of Austria-Hungary and Point XI stipulated that "relations of the several Balkan states to one another be determined by friendly counsel along historically established lines of allegiance and nationality; and for international guarantees of the political and economic independence and territorial integrity of the several Balkan states."

The American delegation's commentary on the revision of Wilson's famous Fourteen Points noted that:

> An internal problem arises out of the refusal of the Croats to accept the domination of the Serbs of the Serbian Kingdom.

In a classic example of diplomatic double-speak the delegation wrote:

> The United States is clearly committed to the programme of national unity and independence. It must stipulate, however, for the protection of national minorities...it supports a programme aiming at a Confederation of Southeastern Europe.

Thus, in the eyes of the victorious Allies, in order to protect the Croatian nation, it was necessary to destroy it.

There was no vote of the Croatian people about their future. By decree, Prince Alexander dissolved the Croatian National Council, convened a Parliament composed primarily of members of the Serbian *Skupština* or Parliament and declared that all laws of the Serbian Constitution of 1903 were in effect throughout the land. Despite the fact that the purpose of the new Yugoslavia was supposed to be the unification of all South Slavs into one state, Serbia, making good on a secret pact with Italy made in 1915, handed over a large part of the land and population of Croatian Dalmatia to Italy, including the strategic cities of Rijeka and Zadar. For the first time in thirteen centuries the ancient Croatian institutions of *Ban* or Viceroy and *Sabor* or Parliament were abolished by the Serbian King. The long process of "Serbianization" had begun.

MYTH:
"A CROATIAN USTAŠE TERRORIST ASSASSINATED KING ALEXANDER"

Myth: King Alexander Karageorgević was assassinated by a Croatian Ustaše terrorist. In an interesting anti-Catholic twist, John Soso, writing in the Hayward, California *Daily Review*, declared that the Croatian assassin fled to and was harbored by the Vatican.

Reality: King Alexander Karageorgević was assassinated by a Macedonian named Vlada Gheorghieff, a member of the Macedonian Revolutionary Organization. Gheorghieff did not flee to the Vatican. He was attacked on the spot by French police and died the evening of the assassination.

This myth was one of the first to be cultivated by Serbian disinformation artists almost immediately after Alexander's death in 1934. Despite the fact that this was the first assassination to be captured on motion picture film and the identity of the gunman was known throughout the world, the "Croatian assassin" myth can be found in encyclopedias and otherwise scholarly works.

Alexander's Yugoslavia

The story of Alexander's death began years earlier when the Croatian pacifist leader Stjepan Radić and four other Croatian leaders were gunned down by a Serbian Deputy on the floor of Parliament. Alexander followed this blow by declaring himself King Dictator on January 6, 1929, abolishing any pretense of constitutionality. Using murder as an instrument of government, he outlawed all political parties, began persecution of Jews and quickly became one of the most hated dictators in Europe.

When the famed Croatian intellectual Milan Šufflay was brutally murdered by Alexander's secret police, even Albert Einstein and Heinrich Mann joined in the international chorus of condemnation of the regime writing in the *New York Times* of May 6, 1931:

> The facts show that cruelty and brutality practiced upon the Croatians only increase...Murder as a political weapon must not be tolerated and political Serbian murderers must not be made national heros.

By 1934, more than 19,000 Croatians had been sentenced to prison for up to twenty years or more and over two hundred had received the death penalty for violations of the draconian catch-all decree known as the "Act for Defense of the Realm." Hundreds more "committed suicide," died of illness in prison or were shot by gendarmes in the "suppression of rebellion." Montenegrins, Slovenes, Macedonians and even democratic Serbs did not fair much better under Alexander's despotic rule.

Having removed all peaceful options for change, Alexander, like Hitler and Mussolini, lived in fear for his life with good cause. From the founding of Serbia in 1804 to the founding of Yugoslavia in 1918, there were eleven

Croatia: Myth and Reality

Vlada Gheorghieff, a member of the Macedonian Revolutionary Organization is struck down by Capt. Piolet, on horseback, moments after the assasination of Alexander. The assasination was the first to be captured on motion picture film.

reigns. Over this 114 year period the average reign was less than ten years. Of all rulers in Serbian history, only two, Miloš and Petar I, died on the throne of natural deaths, and both of them had come to power after being in exile.

The Karageorgević dynasty was founded by Karageorge ("Black George") Petrović, a pig farmer who by his own admission killed 125 men with his own hands, his stepfather and brother among them. He was killed by Miloš in 1817. Black George's son Alexander returned to the throne in 1842 but was deposed by the rival Obrenović "dynasty" and died in exile in 1885. Alexander Obrenović and his queen were in turn murdered in 1903 by Petar I, father of Alexander of Yugoslavia. Alexander came to power only because his older brother Prince George murdered his valet and was forced to renounce his claim to the throne.

Marseilles

The legacy of Serbia's kings, the oppression of Yugoslavia's nationalities and the wrath of those who escaped it came together on October 9, 1934 when the Yugoslav cruiser *Dubrovnik* steamed into the port of Marseilles, France with Alexander on board. His tight-fitting Navy admiral's uniform prevented the King from wearing his customary bullet-proof vest. Alexander had been on French soil less than five minutes when Vlada Gheorghieff mounted the running board of Alexander's car and opened fire with a twenty round Mauser machine pistol, killing the King, French Foreign Minister Louis Barthou and two bystanders. Gheorghieff, a Macedonian by birth and a Bulgarian citizen, was a member of the Macedonian Revolutionary Organization which sought to free Macedonia from Yugoslavia. French Colonel Piolet, mounted on horseback beside the car, immediately drew his saber and attacked Gheorghieff who died later that evening.

The entire event was captured on film and covered by dozens of journalists and witnessed by hundreds of people. Alexander was among the most hated and feared dictators in Europe and a half-dozen or more other would-be assassins of various nationalities were waiting in Marseilles that day. But there is no historical question that a Macedonian-born Bulgarian citizen and member of the Macedonian Revolutionary Movement by the name of Vlada Gheorghieff pulled the trigger, was struck down on the spot, died in custody that evening and was laid to rest in a Marseilles cemetery in the presence of two detectives and a grave digger.

MYTH: "ALL CROATIANS WERE FASCISTS DURING WORLD WAR II; ALL SERBS WERE PRO-ALLIED"

Myth: All Croatians were Fascists during World War II. The Serbian apologist writer Nora Beloff writing in the *Washington Post* may have been the first to add the astounding claim that "all Serbs were pro-Allied."

Reality: Both Croatia and Serbia had pro-Axis governments during World War II. All of the nations of Yugoslavia had elements which supported the Axis and all had elements that were anti-Axis during the War. However, it was the Croatian dominated Partisans, led by the Croatian Josip Broz Tito which formed the only true anti-Fascist fighting force in Yugoslavia and the most formidable Allied force in occupied Europe during World War II.

Flirting with Fascism

World War II came to Yugoslavia as a direct result of the pro-Axis sentiments of the Serbian controlled Yugoslav government. Under Prince Paul Yugoslavia moved steadily away from France and toward Germany after the death of King Alexander. As early as February of 1936 Hitler promised to support the government of Premier Milan Stojadinović.

By 1937 Stojadinović had visited Mussolini, developed his own squad of "Green Shirts" and adopted the Nazi salute. It was perhaps taking the title *Vodja* (*Führer*) that finally sent Prince Paul into action, replacing Stojadinović with Dragiša Cvetković who maintained the same pro-Axis foreign policy but with fewer Fascist trappings.

Prince Paul saw the Third Reich as the only power able to maintain the artificial state of Yugoslavia and he began secret negotiations with top Nazi officials in December 1939. He hoped that he could become King under the New Order, denying the young Crown Prince Peter his title. Yugoslavia joined the Axis on March 24, 1941. The only member of the government who refused to sign the "Pact of Steel" joining the Axis was the Croatian minister, Vladko Maček of the Croatian Peasant Party.

After the signing Cvetković assured Hitler that Yugoslavia "...would be ready to cooperate with Germany in every way." In fact, Paul had been cooperating since 1939 with mass arrests of Jews, strict racial laws, and the prohibition of trade unions. By 1940, legislation had been passed limiting the types of businesses which Jews could own, direct, or work in and severely limiting educational access for Jews. A secret protocol was attached to the Axis pact which promised Yugoslavia access to the Aegean Sea at the expense of Greece in the New Order.

Coup and Invasion

On March 26, 1941 two Serbian generals, Bora Mirković and Dušan Simović, led a British-assisted coup against the Cvetković government. The Anglo-American press went wild with stories about the Serbs' stand against the Axis. In fact, the coup had its roots in both foreign and domestic policy.

Lost in the mythology is the fact that the generals did not think Germany would invade and wanted to maintain cordial relations with the Axis. On March 30 the Yugoslav Foreign Minister made a formal statement to the German envoy that the new government respected the Axis pact and that Simović was "devoted to the maintenance of good and friendly relations with its neighbors the German Reich and the Kingdom of Italy." Simović believed that his close personal friendship with several top Nazis, especially *Reichmarschall* Göring, would save the day. His error led to a German invasion on April 6.

Before seeing a single German soldier, the Serbian-led army withdrew from Slovenia and Croatia to defend Serbia, leaving the Croatians and Slovenes without supplies or ammunition. Most Croatian soldiers simply went home. The Yugoslav military disintegrated at first sight of the Germans as 100 of 135 generals in the top-heavy Serbian officer corps surrendered during the first week. Belgrade was taken by a single platoon of Waffen-SS shock troops led by a second lieutenant on April 12. As General Simović and his government fled the country with millions in gold, only the Croatian Peasant Party minister Vladko Maček stayed to share the fate of his people.

Once a safe distance from the fighting, Simović immediately announced that Yugoslavia had fallen because of the Croatians, all of whom were traitors and Fascists. Ignoring the military abandonment of Croatia and Slovenia, the mass surrender of the Serbian officer corps, and the obvious fact that the entire government had fled, Simović announced that Serbia had been stabbed in the back.

The Yugoslav ambassador to the United States, Konstatin Fotić, worked overtime spreading the tale that Yugoslavia had been defeated only because of Croatian disloyalty, despite the fact that his cousin headed the new pro-Nazi government in Serbia and that another cousin was leader of the Serbian Nazi Party.

The Croatian State

Croatia was occupied by Germany and Italy and divided into German and Italian occupation zones. The Independent State of Croatia was established with the consent of Germany and against the expressed wishes of Italy which wanted to make it an Italian Kingdom. Italy went so far as to name a "King of Croatia" who never set foot in his erstwhile kingdom. The Croatian government was led by Ante Pavelić and his *Ustaše* movement.

Pavelić had been an elected Deputy in Parliament and vice-president of the Croatian Bar Association when Alexander declared the dictatorship and dissolved Parliament. Pavelić founded the *Ustaše* in exile with the aim of liberating Croatia by force. When war broke out, underground *Ustaše* throughout Croatia took control of the government well before the Germans arrived. As in the Soviet Union, when the Germans did arrive, they were at first welcomed as liberators.

The new Croatian government adopted German racial and economic laws and persecuted Jews, Serbs, Communists, Peasant Party leaders and others. While fighting primarily for its own survival against Serbian *Četniks* who wanted to restore the Serbian monarchy and the Communist-led Partisans, the Croatian State joined the Axis and later sent troops to the Russian front.

While the majority of the Croatian people favored an independent Croatian state, many did not support the *Ustaše* regime. When the war broke out there were fewer than twelve thousand members of the movement representing less than one per cent of the Croatian population. At its height in 1942, there were only sixty thousand *Ustaše*. Over sixty per cent were from impoverished Western Herzegovina with a strong anti-Serbian sentiment from the dictatorship of Alexander. Some twenty per cent were Muslims who joined in direct response to Serbian massacres in Bosnia. The leader of Croatia's popular Peasant Party was jailed by the regime during the War.

Many members of the Croatian officer corps were pro-Allied and supported the Croatian Peasant Party. In September 1944 pro-Allied officers attempted a *coup* against Pavelić. The plotters had been promised an Anglo-American landing in Dalmatia and would have turned the Croatian Army against Germany to support the Allied invasion. The landing never took place. Dr. Ivan Šubašić of the Yugoslav Government-in-Exile learned of the plot and informed the Soviets. Stalin immediately contacted Roosevelt and informed him that any such action would be a violation of the Tehran agreement dividing Europe into spheres of influence. Roosevelt cancelled all plans for the landing but British secret channels withheld the information from the Croatians on the premise that any revolt, even one doomed to failure, was better for the Allied cause than nothing.

Serbia and the Četniks

In Serbia, a new pro-Nazi government was first established under the leadership of Milan Asimović and later under former Minister of War General Milan Nedić which governed until 1945. Nedić supported Hitler and met with him in 1943. This new government established even

Serbian postage stamps of 1941. Belgrade was the first city in Europe to be declared *Judenfrei*; free of Jews. The Serbian insignia, still used today, appears in the upper corner of each stamp.

harsher racial laws than Prince Paul had enacted and immediately established three concentration camps for Jews, Gypsies and others. Nedić formed his own paramilitary storm troops known as the State Guard. The Guard was comprised of former members of the Četniks which had existed as an all-Serbian para-military police force under Alexander and Paul to enforce loyalty from non-Serbian members of the armed forces.

When Yugoslavia disintegrated, one faction of Četniks swore allegiance to the new Serbian Nazi government. Another group remained under the pre-war leader Kosta Pećanac who openly collaborated with the Germans. A third Četnik faction followed the Serbian Fascist Dimitrije Ljotić. Ljotić's units were primarily responsible for tracking down Jews, Gypsies and Partisans for execution or deportation to concentration camps. By August 1942 the Serbian government would proudly announce that Belgrade was the first city in the New Order to be *Judenfrei* or "free of Jews." Only 1,115 of Belgrade's twelve thousand Jews would survive. Ninty-five per cent of the Jewish population of Serbia was exterminated.

Still other Četniks rallied behind Draža Mihailović, a 48 year-old Army officer who had been court-martialed by Nedić and was known to have close ties to Britain. Early in the War Mihailović offered some resistance to the German forces while collaborating with the Italians. By July 22, 1941 the Yugoslav Government-in-Exile announced that continued resistance was impossible.

Although Mihailović and his exiled government would maintain a fierce propaganda campaign to convince the Allies that his Četniks were inflicting great damage on the Axis, the Četniks did little for the war effort and openly collaborated with the Germans and Italians while fighting the *Ustaše* and Partisans. At its peak, Mihailović's Četniks claimed to have three hundred thousand troops. In fact they never numbered over thirty-one thousand.

Mihailović was executed in 1946 for treason. The extent of *Četnik* collaboration with the German and Italian armies as well as their vicious war against the pro-Allied Partisans is well documented in dozens of books, including Professor J. Tomasevich's scholarly and definitive work *The Chetniks*.

The Partisans

The Partisans, founded by Josip Broz Tito, a Croatian Communist, represented the only true resistance to the Axis in Yugoslavia during World War II. Hundreds of thousands of Croatians joined the Partisans and thirty-nine of the Partisan's eighty brigades were Croatian. On June 22, 1941 Croatian Partisans began what would come to be known as the War of Liberation in Yugoslavia.

On July 13, 1943 a Democratic Republic of Croatia under the leadership of Andrija Hebrang was declared in those areas occupied by the Croatian Partisan forces. As the war progressed more and more Croatians, especially from Dalmatia, joined the Partisans. Serbs joined in great numbers late in the War as entire *Četnik* units changed their allegiance. By 1943 Allied support shifted to Tito and by 1944 the Partisans were the only recognized Allied force fighting in Yugoslavia.

The complexities of World War II saw Croatian fighting Croatian, Serb fighting Serb, and both fighting each other as well as German, Italian, Hungarian and Bulgarian forces. Both Serbia and Croatia, like Finland, Hungary, France and virtually every other nation in Europe, were occupied by the Axis and had governments which collaborated with the Axis. Both Croatia and Serbia also had Partisan governments fighting for the Allies. A half century later Germany and Japan were again great world powers and Italy was a full partner in the European community while Croatia, having been occupied by Germany and Italy, continued to be tarred with the brush of Fascism by Belgrade's mythology.

MYTH:
"THE BASKET OF HUMAN EYEBALLS"

Myth: The Croatian wartime Chief-of-State Ante Pavelić routinely maintained a basket containing twenty kilos of human eyeballs at his desk side.

Reality: This statement is literally a work of fiction taken from the novel *Kaputt* by Curzio Malaparte (Kurt Suckert, also known as Gianni Strozzi). The book was written as fiction, sold as fiction, and is cataloged in every library in the world as fiction. To cite *Kaputt* as a source about World War II is analogous to citing *Gone With the Wind* as an authoritative history of the American Civil War.

That this tired tale is still being retold is the second most amazing part of this myth. More amazing is that anybody, no matter how blinding their hatred of Croatians, could believe it. And yet this myth was quoted as fact as recently as 1991 in official publications printed in Belgrade by the Ministry of Information of the Republic of Serbia and repeated by naive journalists in Britain and North America.

Kaputt

The myth survived and was given renewed life by the Serbian government, journalists and politicians because it came with quotation marks. The legend had a footnote, a citation, an author and all the trappings of fact. The author was often cited as "the most famous Italian writer," "the Italian journalist" and even the "famed Italian historian," Curzio Malaparte. His famous quote from the 1946 English translation of the novel *Kaputt* reads:

> While he spoke, I gazed at a wicker basket on the Poglavnik's desk. The lid was raised and the basket seemed to be filled with mussels, or shelled oysters --as they are occasionally displayed in the windows of Fortnum and Mason in Piccadilly in London.
>
> Castertano looked at me and winked, "Would you like a nice oyster stew?"
>
> "Are they Dalmatian oysters?" I asked the Poglavnik.
>
> Ante Pavelič removed the lid from the basket and revealed the mussels, that slimy and jelly-like mass, and he said smiling, with that tired good-natured smile of his, "It is a present from my loyal *ustashis*. Forty pounds of human eyes. *

Kaputt and its author both had fascinating stories to tell. In the original press release for the book, Malaparte claimed that the manuscript was started in the Ukraine in 1941 and smuggled throughout Europe in secret coat linings and in the soles of his shoes. Finally, the manuscript was divided into three parts and given to three diplomats, to be reunited in 1943 on Capri where it was finished.

* *Poglavnik* was Ante Pavelić's title.

The book chronicled Malaparte's movements around Europe in 1941 and 1942 when he visited every front and knew every head of state, usually on a first name basis. Malaparte apparently spoke every language and shared the charms of every beautiful princess on the continent.

According to his own preface to *Kaputt*, his personal friendships with Mussolini, Hitler and others did not save him from being thrown into jail in July 1943 for being anti-German. Miraculously, he was soon freed and was working for the Allies by September of that year. It was while working as a propagandist for the Allies that Malaparte completed *Kaputt*, a book which he described as "...horribly gay and gruesome."

The critics agreed. Malaparte's two major books, *Kaputt* and *Skin* were labeled "Best selling Nausea" by *Time* magazine which christened Malaparte as "...a sort of Jean Paul Spillane." Malaparte's writings contained page after page of sordid tales about the evil world of Fascist Europe. Malaparte's basket of human eyeballs must be taken in context, as *Time* magazine wrote in 1952:

> He shows mothers who sell their children into prostitution; but then, says Malaparte with a smirk, there are also the children who would gladly sell their mothers. He dwells for part of a chapter on a street peopled with twisted female dwarfs, who fed, he asserts gleefully, on the unnatural lust in the American ranks. Another chapter is concerned with a visit to a shop that sells blonde pubic wigs. U.S. soldiers, Malaparte explains, like blondes.

These offensive themes only scratch the surface of Malaparte's sick writings. That the Allies won the War through the devices of a "homosexual maquis," flags of human skin, and an Allied general who served his guests a boiled child are all included in Malaparte's fare.

Suckert-Malaparte-Strozzi

"Malaparte" himself was an enigma. He was born Kurt Erich Suckert in 1898 in Prato, Italy of Austrian, Russian and Italian descent. He attended the *Collegio Cicognini* and the University of Rome. He joined the Fascists at an early age and soon became the darling of the Fascist Propaganda Ministry where he wrote glowing volumes and even a work of poetry in praise of Mussolini. He served as a journalist for *Corriere della Sera* and travelled to Ethiopia in 1939.

What happened after that depends upon which "Malaparte" is read. The world-travelling statesman fictionalized in his novels spent the war years in almost constant meetings with the likes of Mussolini, Count Ciano, Ante Pavelić and the rich and powerful of Europe. Interestingly, Pavelić's name was misspelled "Pavelič" in all of his writings.

Later, Malaparte claimed to have been one of "three Italian officers who organized the Italian Army of Liberation which fought for the Allies." After the fall of Mussolini he began writing under the name Gianni Strozzi for the Communist daily *L'Unita*. That year he applied for, but was refused, Communist Party membership. Still later, he went to work for the Allied Fifth Army Headquarters as a minor liaison officer. Just as he had served the Fascists and the Communists, Malaparte sought to ingratiate himself with his new masters. "The American Army is the kindest army in the world...I like Americans...and I proved it a hundred times during the war...their souls are pure, much purer than ours," Malaparte gushed.

In November of 1952 a far different Malaparte wrote that in fact he had fallen out with Mussolini in 1934. Not only did he never meet most of the great leaders he wrote about, he admitted: "In 1938 I still remained under police control and was put in prison as a preventative measure every time a Nazi chief visited Rome...and from 1933 until the liberation, I was deprived of a passport..."

Once called "Fascism's Strongest Pen," Malaparte angered Hitler with a book written in 1931 about the techniques of the *coup d' etat*. He was jailed by Mussolini from 1933 to 1938 and kept on a very short leash for the remainder of the Fascist era.

While a prolific author of short stories and fictionalized accounts of Fascist victories, it is doubtful that Suckert-Malaparte-Strozzi ever set foot in Croatia during the War. The Italian Defense Ministry did confirm that he once served as a liaison officer to the Allies, but flatly denied that he had anything to do with organizing Italy's Army of Liberation.

After the War, Malaparte continued to write, as well as direct and produce movies, and was active in the Communist Party. In the Spring of 1975 the Party sent him on a comradely visit to China. Shortly after his return, he died on July 19, 1957. An enigma to the end, the viciously anti-Catholic Malaparte renounced Communism and converted to Catholicism on his death bed. Malaparte and his unpleasant fiction have been relegated to the dust bin of literary history in all of the world except Belgrade.

MYTH:
"TWO MILLION SERBS DIED"

Myth: Between 500,000 and 2,000,000 Serbs were murdered by the Croatian government during World War II.

Reality: The exact number of war victims in Yugoslavia during World War II may never be known due to fifty years of intentional disinformation by the Yugoslavian and Serbian governments, Serbian exile groups, and others. However, it is likely that approximately one million people of all nationalities died of war-related causes in all of Yugoslavia during World War II and that as many as 125,000 Serbs died of war-related causes in Croatia during the War.

The question of war losses during World War II represents the most divisive, heated and emotional issue among all of the nationalities of the former Yugoslavia during the post-War period. The bloody multi-sided War in Yugoslavia involved the German, Italian, *Ustaše*, Partisan, *Domobran*, White Guard, Slovenian Guard and at least four different Četnik armies. The multifaceted war pitted Serbs against Serbs, Croatians against Croatians, Serbs against Croatians, and Serbian Orthodox against Catholics and Muslims. The loss of life was heavy and difficult to document. As the war progressed and even long after the war ended, the mythology of the numbers of victims continued to grow.

The Growing Numbers

On the question of the number of Serbs killed in Croatia, it became possible to simply pick a number and virtually any press medium in the world would publish the figure without question. In one sixty day period in late 1991, David Martin put the number at 500,000 in the *New York Times*; Serbian President Slobodan Milošević at 750,000 in *USA Today*; Josif Djordjevich at 1,200,000 in the *San Francisco Chronicle*; Teddy Preuss at 1,500,000 in the *Jerusalem Post*; and, setting an all-time record, Peter Jennings' *ABC News* program set the figure at a record 2,000,000. Further, each of the sources added a separate twist to the number. For some, the number represented total "killed," for others "murdered," others "murdered in concentration camps," and still others did not define how the losses occurred. None listed any source for the figures.

To illustrate the magnitude of these charges, it would require killing one person every 90 seconds, 24 hours a day, 7 days a week for the entire duration of the War to reach Mr. Preuss' figure of 1,500,000. The fact is one million people did not die in Croatia from all causes during the War. Many scholars doubt that there were a million lives lost to war-related causes in all of Yugoslavia during World War II.

Yet this mythology runs deeper than virtually any other. As early as April 1942 the Serbian Orthodox Church in America, based upon Mihailović's reports, claimed that over one million Serbs had already been killed in Croatia. As the war progressed, the numbers continued to grow in the Serbian press until actually exceeding the number of Serbs in Croatia. It must be noted that no Croatian troops set foot in Serbia during World War II. Thus all accounting of Serbian losses must be for those living in Croatia, Bosnia and Hercegovnia.

Post-War Accountability

After World War II, the Communist Yugoslav government set the total demographic losses for all of Yugoslavia from all causes at 1,700,000. The figure was never verified and was contradicted by demographic data comparisons between the Yugoslav census of 1931 and 1948. Nevertheless, this figure, which included natural mortality and decreased birth rate, was presented to the West German government for war reparations.

At the same time, the Belgrade media began circulation of the figure 750,000 Jews, Gypsies and Serbs killed in Croatia during the War. By 1958 the number 750,000 was used to describe losses at a single camp, Jasenovac. Such high numbers were used not only to gain additional war reparations from Germany, but also to legitimatize the Communist governments' role in saving the peoples of Yugoslavia from the horrors of nationalism.

Germany refused to accept the 1.7 million figure and demanded documentation. On June 10, 1964 the Yugoslav government secretly ordered that the exact statistics regarding war victims be assembled. The task was completed in the Socialist Republic of Croatia by the Center for the Scientific Documentation of the Institute for the History of the Worker's Movement in Zagreb. By early November, the data had been collected and were sent to the Federal Institute for Statistics in Belgrade.

When the data were tabulated, excluding Axis forces, the actual figure was 597,323 deaths for all of Yugoslavia. Of these, 346,740 were Serbians and 83,257 were Croatians for all of Yugoslavia. These figures excluded the deaths of any person who died fighting for the *Četniks*, *Ustaše*, regular Croatian Army, Slovenian Home Guards or serving in the German or Italian Armies. The government returned the data for retabulation and the figures were confirmed and provided to Germany.

The Data Made Public

In July of 1969, Bruno Bušić, an associate at the Center for Scientific Documentation, published data from the 1964 study showing that 185,327 people were thought to have died of all causes in Croatia during the War and that 64,245 may have died in German or Croatian prisons or concentration camps. In September of that year the magazine that published the data was banned and Bušić was arrested in 1971. After serving two years in prison he escaped to Paris where he wrote several monographs on political prisoners in Croatia. He was murdered in Paris in October 1978 by the Yugoslav Secret Police.

In 1985, the Serbian scholar Bogoljub Kočović published a major scholarly research work which put the figure for total demographic losses in all of Yugoslavia at 1,985,000 of which 971,000 were war-related. Of these 487,000 were Serbs killed anywhere in Yugoslavia by any side including Germans, Italians, Croatians, Albanians, Hungarians, Soviets, American bombing or by other Serbs. Kočović concluded that some 125,000 Serbs and 124,000 Croatians died in Croatia during World War II. Kočović also noted what many previous demographers had ignored. The first post-war census was taken in 1948 and "it is fully justified to take into account these post-war victims of communist terror," in reference to the thousands of Croatians slaughtered in late 1945 and 1946 in what have come to be called the Bleiburg Massacres.

In 1989 The Yugoslav Victimological Society and the Zagreb Jewish Community published what is now considered the definitive work by Vladimir Žerjavić which set total war losses at 1,027,000 of which 530,000 were Serbs and 192,000 Croatians. 131,000 Serbs and 106,000 Croatians were listed as having died of all war-related causes in Croatia.

The Myth Grows On

Regardless of which scholarly study is consulted, no study has ever reached the figures so casually thrown about in the media. And despite all scholarly evidence to the contrary, in 1992 the Serbian Ministry of Information in Belgrade continued to claim that 600,000 Serbs were killed and the President of Serbia claimed 750,000 were killed by the Croatians during World War II. The Western media, unfettered by any need for factual documentation not only published these numbers, but, as in the case of *ABC News*, increased them by over one million victims.

The Serbian scholar Bogoljub Kočović best summarized the dilemma of those who would dare to seek the truth in this complex and volatile history:

> Very soon it dawned upon me that the major obstacle to my work would be the myths created over four decades about the number of victims; myths by now deeply implanted in the soul of the people of all religions, political beliefs and nationality; myths which, by repetition became a 'reality'. There will be many who will reject my study because it does not conform to their beliefs...Many of them are looking for spiritual food to ignite their hatred of the Croats.

MYTH:
"THE CROATIANS EXECUTED DOZENS OF AMERICAN AIRMEN"

Myth: The Croatian government during World War II had a policy of executing downed Allied airmen and dozens of American airmen were executed by the Croatians during the War.

Reality: The Croatian government, signatory to the Geneva Conventions, had no policy of executing captured airmen of any nationality. There is no evidence that any American airman was executed by the Croatian government during World War II. There is considerable evidence that Allied prisoners of war in Croatia were very well treated in captivity.

Almost unique among myths, it is possible to actually trace the origin of this story back to its source; the Balkan Intelligence Chief.

> At INS headquarters in Los Angeles, kept under lock and key and marked "secret" is the file of Andrija Artukovic...According to the testimony of one American Intelligence chief in the Balkans section during the Second World War, he also approved orders that sent dozens of American pilots to firing squads.

Reader's Digest

The preceeding quotation made its international debut in the December 1973 issue of *Reader's Digest* magazine in a small unattributed "box" within a larger article on illegal immigration. *Reader's Digest* is often cited despite the fact that no author or source was given. Like most myths, it has since taken on a life of its own and more recent versions have added the "official policy of the Croatian government."

When asked to name the "American Intelligence chief" or cite their sources, the editors of *Reader's Digest* first claimed that the article had been "carefully checked by our research and legal departments and we believe they found adequate support for all the factual statements." Despite hundreds of requests from scholars, political leaders, Accuracy in Media and others, the magazine was never able to produce the name of the intelligence officer or any evidence that a single American was executed by the Croatian government during the War.

By April of 1974, *Reader's Digest* began referring all inquires to their legal department. Finally on March 25, 1974 the editors, responding to a formal request by California State Assemblyman Doug Carter, admitted that the charges were "...claims and allegations, not necessarily fully documented facts."

The Balkan Intelligence Chief

The myth did not originate with the *Reader's Digest* in 1973 however. The identity of the "Balkan Intelligence Chief" can be traced back to the June 26, 1958 edition of a small California newspaper, the *Palos Verdes News*. On that date John J. Knezevich, the Serbian-American publisher of the paper wrote:

> During the last war, I was head of the Balkin (*sic*) section of the United States Army and Navy Joint Intelligence Collection Agency...I know whereof I am speaking.

Knezevich went on to accuse Artuković of no fewer than 740,000 deaths including the deaths of "dozens of American pilots." This was not Knezevich's first article on the subject. He had made the charges in his newspaper as early as May 17, 1951. Whether Mr. Knezevich held any post with the intelligence community during World War II is not known. However, it seems implausible that a Chief of Balkan intelligence would have consistently misspelled the word "Balkin" in all of his writings. What is known about Knezevich is that he was active in several Serbian organizations in southern California and was active in any number of anti-Croatian and anti-Catholic movements of the 1950s. His newspaper column "Review of Events" was a regular front-page feature often filled with anti-Tito, anti-Communist, anti-Croatian and anti-Catholic propaganda.

Knezevich is first mentioned in the extradition case of Andrija Artuković, a wartime Croatian cabinet minister wanted by Tito for crimes against the state. On May 8, 1951 Knezevich asked to appear *in camera* before the Immigration and Naturalization Examiner. He presented "confidential" information that he had seen documents signed by Artuković ordering the execution of dozens of pilots. Under examination however, Knezevich refused to state whether he had ever been anywhere in the Balkans during the War; what he had done, if anything, in the military; and generally refused to answer direct questions.

The INS Examiner discounted his testimony and none of it was ever presented nor was the charge concerning American pilots ever mentioned in any future proceedings in the United States or Yugoslavia from 1951 until 1986. Obviously, the American and Yugoslav governments would not have passed up such an important witness or such a charge had they found the slightest shred of evidence to support his story.

Knezevich penned the final chapter of the story on July 24, 1958 when he listed all of the charges that he had made against Artuković, including the execution of American pilots, wrote: "Inasmuch as neither the writer or publisher are in a position to prove independently the truth or falsity of these assertions, they are all and singularly retracted. (signed) Palos Verdes News John J. Knezevich." Knezevich died in 1965.

The Airmen and the Baroness

Learning the realities of the fate of American airmen in Croatia during World War II proved even more interesting than uncovering the source of the mythology. Between the years of 1973 and 1979, this author undertook primary and secondary research into the subject which resulted in a monograph titled *Allied Prisoners of War in Croatia 1941-1945*. Since there were fewer than one hundred airmen, American, British, Russian, South African, and Partisan, who were held by the Croatian government during the War, the myth that "dozens" or twenty-five per cent, were executed is a significant one.

As a part of the study, ten Americans who had been held prisoner-of-war in Croatia were interviewed as were guards, the American-born priest who celebrated mass and others who were present at the estate of the Baroness Nikolić which served as the POW "camp" on the outskirts of Zagreb. The findings of this study were surprising. It was learned that the "camp" at 203 Pantovcak in Zagreb had no fence. Visitors were welcome and some POWs visited a nearby tavern until German soldiers visited the same tavern. POWs had a radio and listened to U.S. Armed Forces radio. And the camp tennis champion was Frank Ryan of Sommerville, New Jersey.

Essentially the Baroness Nikolić considered the airmen her guests and afforded them the best treatment and food available given the wartime conditions, including a generous wine ration. Several POWs worked in the villa's vineyards and records were kept of all such work so that the POWs could be paid after the war as provided for by Geneva Conventions. Given the chaotic state at the end of the war, the airmen were given vouchers instead of cash. One former POW, a guest of honor at a Los Angeles Croatian Day celebration in 1979, still had his voucher and promised to cash it in when Croatia became independent.

Often the Croatian Red Cross provided the airmen with such luxuries as chocolate and cigarettes that were

Baroness Nikolic, Fr. Benkovic, holding an American airman's hat, the camp commander, in great coat and American, British and South African POWs at the Nikolic "camp" in Zagreb.

Four Croatian guards, one visiting Croatian civilian and American POWs at the Nikolic "camp" near Zagreb.

unavailable to the average Croatian soldier. While wounded or ill Croatian soldiers could expect little more than meager supplies in field first aid stations, American POWs were treated at Zagreb's finest hospital and there is photographic evidence of visits to them by Croatian Chief-of-State Pavelić and other officials.

Americans Helping Croatians

In early 1945 an attempt was made to evacuate American pilots from what was soon to be a war zone. Croatian Air Force General Rubčić saw to it that twelve American pilots were trained in the use of Croatian aircraft, planes which represented the last hope for the air defense of Croatia's capital. After familiarization, fourteen Americans and one Croatian liaison officer flew to Allied Italy via Zadar where they tried to convince American forces to land on the Dalmatian coast and meet the Red Army at the Drina river. In 1943 Croatian Lt. Colonel Ivan Babić had flown a similar mission to American occupied Italy to suggest to the Americans that such an invasion would meet no resistance and that the Croatian Army would even establish a beachhead for them. The American command knew that the Dalamatian coast was Hitler's great weakness and that such an attack could split the German armies. Neither the Croatian nor American commanders knew that Yugoslavia had been designated as the Soviet sphere by Roosevelt, Churchill and Stalin. Allied forces continued to fight and die one foot at a time up the boot of Italy.

Still other Americans offered their services to the Croatians in order to try to save Croatian troops from the communists. Lt. Edward J. Benkoski, pilot of the P-38 fighter "Butch," joined Englishman Rodney Woods and John Gray, a Scot, in attempting to negotiate for the Croatians in May 1945. Another American officer accompanied Croatian officials to negotiations at Bleiburg, Austria at the end of the war to keep Croatians from being returned to certain death in Yugoslavia. They failed.

The American priest Theodore Benković who often celebrated mass for the airmen wrote:

> Despite constant American bombings, the Croatians bore no hatred toward the Americans, for in a fatalistic way they held it to be necessary. I saw my countrymen held captive in Mostar, how the people treated them well, even offering the American flyers the few cigarettes they possessed; how they begged me to make known to my countrymen of their hope of liberation by the Americans.

None of the airmen interviewed or surveyed recalled any instance of mistreatment and some provided documentary and photographic evidence of very close personal relationships with Croatian officers and female members of the Croatian Red Cross. The study failed to find the name of any Allied POW who was executed and found no "official policy" of executing airmen. Several airmen did recall that they were warned in pre-flight briefings that they would be executed if captured by the Croatians. That information was supplied by Mihailović's Serbian Četniks who were paid in gold for each airman returned to the Allies.

In January 1966 the Baroness Nikolić visited the United States to attend a showing of her artworks. Several of her former "prisoners" welcomed her to Cleveland. One, Gene Keck of Washta, Iowa travelled nine hundred miles by bus to see her again. "She's my second mother...I was her baby when we were on her estate in Zagreb." Often the mythology is diametrically opposite of the truth.

MYTH:
"THERE WAS NO RETRIBUTION AGAINST THE CROATIANS AFTER WORLD WAR II"

Myth: Because Tito was a Croatian, no retribution was taken against Croatian officials, soldiers or civilians after World War II by the victorious Partisans.

Reality: Thousands of Croatians were slaughtered immediately after the War, tens of thousands more were sent to prisons, government officials were executed and those who escaped were tracked down and murdered in foreign lands well into the 1960s.

That there was no retribution against the Croatians after World War II is not so much a myth as an outright attempt to falsify history. As is the case with several other myths, the Serbian apologists Nora Beloff and David Martin gave new currency to this story in the world press during the Croatian war for independence.

Bleiburg

The post-war massacres of Croatians are almost unknown outside the Croatian community. To Croatians, the single word "Bleiburg" summarizes the pain endured by an entire nation. The Bleiburg-Maribor massacres have been documented in such works as *Operation Slaughterhouse* by John Prcela and Stanko Guldescu, *In Tito's Death Marches and Extermination Camps* by Joseph Hečimović, *Operation Keelhaul* by Julius Epstein, *Bleiburg* by Vinko Nikolić, and perhaps best known, *The Minister and the Massacres* by Count Nikolai Tolstoy. That these massacres occurred is irrefutable. Only the number of deaths and the depth of American and British duplicity are in question.

The story of Bleiburg began in early 1945 as it became clear that Germany would lose the War. As the German Army retreated toward the Austrian border, the Red Army advanced and the Partisans began their consolidation of power, anarchy prevailed in what was Yugoslavia. A dozen or more nationalist movements and ethnic militias attempted to salvage various parts of Yugoslavia. Most nationalists, Croatian, Slovenian and Serbian alike, were anti-Communist and all had visions of the Western Allies welcoming them into the coming battle against Communism. Croatians especially cherished the totally unsupported notion that Anglo-American intervention would save an independent Croatian state.

As in every other part of eastern Europe, armies, governments and civilian populations began moving toward the Western lines. Some were pushed before the retreating Germans, others followed in their wake. Many travelled in small bands, armed or unarmed, while others were well organized into mass movements of people and equipment. Along the trek north they fought the Partisans and each other. Many surrendered, others fought to the death.

Retreat from Zagreb

The retreating Germans, usually without bothering to inform their erstwhile allies, took with them much of the material support for the Croatian armed forces. Despite conditions, several Croatian generals wanted to defend the city of Zagreb from the Partisan advance and fight to the finish if necessary. The Partisans made it clear that the city, swollen to twice its size with refugees, would be destroyed if they met resistance. A final meeting of the Croatian government was held on April 30, 1945 at which the decision was made to abandon Zagreb and retreat into Austria.

Still quite naive concerning Allied intentions, many Croatian officers hoped that the still sizable Croatian Army would be allowed to surrender to the British to fight again against the Russians. Since both Croatia and Britain were signatories to the Geneva Conventions, it was felt that at worst the Croatians would be treated as prisoners of war.

The exodus from Zagreb began on May 1st. Some 200,000 civilians were flanked by 200,000 soldiers, sailors and airmen of the Croatian armed forces. The Archbishop-Metropolitan Aloysius Stepinac took charge of the government for the few hours between the departure of Croatian officials and the arrival of the Partisan Liberation Army. State Minister Vrančić was dispatched to Italy as a peace emissary to the Allies and several high-ranking English speaking officers headed the main column toward Austria.

The retreat was well ordered and the protecting flank armies insured that all of the civilians arrived safely at the Austrian border by May 7. A number of military units remained behind to fight delaying actions as late as May 12. Still other units, known as "Crusaders" fled into the hills and fought sporadic guerilla actions until 1948.

The huge column, numbering perhaps as many as one-half million soldiers and civilians, including Slovenes, Serbs and even Četnik units, finally came to rest in a small valley near the Austrian village of Bleiburg.

The leaders had no way of knowing that their peace emissary, Dr. Vrančić had travelled as far as Forli, Italy by plane and car under a white flag only to be stopped short of his goal. At Forli, Vrančić and Naval Captain Vrkljan, who spoke fluent English, were detained by one Captain Douglas of British Field Security who was more interested in their diplomatic grade Mercedes-Benz automobile than their mission to see Field Marshal Alexander in Caserta. He held the emissaries incommunicado until May 20 when he had them thrown into a POW camp and confiscated the automobile.

Deception and Betrayal

In the belief that their envoys had made some arrangement with the British, the multitude of humanity set up camp in the valley to await the outcome of negotiations. One of the first groups to arrive at British headquarters was a contingent of 130 members of the Croatian government headed by President Nikola Mandić. All were told that they would be transferred to Italy as soon as possible by British Military Police. All were then loaded into a train and returned to the Partisans for execution. It was the intent of the British to turn over all Croatians, as well as Serbs and Slovenes, to the Communists from whom they had fled.

When the Croatian military leaders realized that they had led hundreds of thousands into a trap, many committed suicide on the spot. The British extradited at first hundreds, then thousands of Croatians. Some were shot at the border, while others joined the infamous "Death Marches" which took them deeper into the new People's Republic for liquidation.

Realizing the importance of the clergy to the Croatian people, most church leaders were arrested. Although Archbishop Stepinac was sentenced to death, he was saved by a massive outcry of world public opinion and died under house arrest in 1960. Two bishops, three hundred priests, twenty-nine seminarians and four lay brothers were less fortunate and were executed.

The number of Muslim religious leaders executed has never been determined, although the figure is thought to be in excess of six hundred. Churches and mosques were closed or destroyed throughout Croatia and Bosnia-Hercegovina. The new government dynamited the minarets around the mosque of Zagreb, turned the building into a museum glorifying the Partisan victory and renamed the square in which it stood "Victims of Fascism Square." One of the first acts of the Croatian government in 1991 was to rename the plaza.

Almost every government official from the President to local postmasters, every military officer above the rank of major and virtually every *Ustaše* officer, regardless of rank, was found guilty of "crimes against the people." Many were executed. Enlisted members of the *Ustaše* were often found guilty *en masse* and sent to concentration camps where many died. All top ranking members of the government were executed. Chief-of-state Ante Pavelić managed to flee only to be gunned down by a would-be assassin in 1957. He later died of complications.

Denial and Discovery

The total number of people liquidated may never be known, but figures of 100 to 180 thousand have been voiced by some, up to one-quarter of a million by others. Despite the scholarship and masses of documents proving the contrary, the Yugoslav government denied that the Bleiburg-Maribor massacres or any subsequent liquidation of anti-Communists occurred. As late as 1976 special teams were active in Slovenia and southern Austria covering up evidence of the crimes. The American and British governments, implicated in the forced repatriation that led to the slaughter also sought to cover-up or at least ignore the crimes.

Finally, in July of 1990 with the departure of the Communist regime, the truth began to come to light. In underground caverns in Slovenia and northern Croatia, researchers using spelunker's equipment descended into the mass graves long before sealed by the authorities. They found layer upon layer of human bones, crutches, rope and wire. Many of the skulls had a single bullet hole in the back. Estimates ranged from 5,000 victims in one cave to as many as 40,000 in another. When news was made public, people from throughout Croatia and Slovenia reported other mass grave sites that had been known to them for years. For obvious reasons none had ever spoken publicly of them before.

In 1990 the Croatian Parliament formed a commission which included foreign experts to determine, for the first time, the full extent of the post-war massacres. Determining how many perished will be a difficult undertaking that will require years of grizzly exploration and detailed research. Whatever the final result, it will never again be said that Croatia did not suffer in post-war Yugoslavia.

MYTH:
"BORDERS WERE DRAWN TO BENEFIT CROATIA"

Myth: The Serbian-Croatian border was drawn up secretly by Tito, a Croatian, in 1943 benefiting Croatia at the expense of Serbia.

Reality: Croatia's border with Serbia is essentially the same as in 1848 and 1918 with the exception of those lands taken from Croatia and given to Serbia and Montenegro under both Yugoslav regimes.

This mythology is a recent creation of the Serbian government and has been given wide circulation by Serbian apologists Nora Beloff and David Martin. The purpose of the myth is to stress to the world that the borders of the former Yugoslav republics are simply administrative boundaries with no historical significance. Once this myth is taken as fact the argument follows that such meaningless borders are subject to negotiation and change, in favor of Serbia.

The reality is that Croatia today has roughly the same borders as in 1848. Serbia has increased its borders after every one of its many wars since 1813. Today Serbia controls more territory than it has in its entire history. In the north it has annexed the lands of the Hungarians and Croatians. In the south two hundred thousand Serbs rule over two million ethnic Albanians in the absolute police state of Kosova. Montenegro has become nothing more than a Serbian province.

The myth that Serbian lands are held by Croatia was used by the Serbian government to launch a war of aggression to seize valuable gas and oil fields, rail and shipping corridors and port facilities. Eastern Slavonia, where Serbian aggression resulted in the total devastation of the ancient city of Vukovar, had a Serbian population of 16.4% according to the 1991 census. Dubrovnik, which underwent months of siege by Serbian forces, had a Serbian population of only 6.2% in 1991. Neither region has ever been a part of Serbia.

Croatia's Borders

The borders of Croatia have changed over the past thousand years reflecting the ebbs and flows of the great empires around her. When King Tomislav united Pannonian and Dalmatian Croatia in 925, the Byzantine Emperor Constantine Porphyrogenitus recorded that Croatia covered some 100,000 square kilometers (38,600 square miles), had a population in excess of two million and fielded 60,000 horsemen, 100,000 foot soldiers, 80 galleys and one hundred cutters, a formidable state for tenth century Europe.

Serbians at that time were under the control of Bulgar or Byzantine rulers and did not organize their first state until in 1170. Serbia reached its zenith under Czar Stephen Dušan who died in 1355. His death was followed by civil war among Serbian nobles which led to a Turkish invasion. The Serbs suffered a stunning defeat at the battle of Kosova in 1389 and another at Smederevo in 1459. Serbia remained only as an Ottoman vassal state well into the nineteenth century when it was fully reestablished as an independent state by the Treaty of Berlin in 1878.

The expansion of the Ottoman Empire in the fifteenth century also had tremendous effect on the size and character of Croatia. The Croatian lands of Bosnia and Hercegovina were absorbed by the Ottomans in 1463 and 1482, reducing Croatia to a 16,000 square mile crescent protecting Europe from the Turks. In 1699 the Habsburgs recovered all of Croatia and Slavonia and settled Germans and a large number of fleeing Serbs into Slavonia and Vojvodina. Upon the defeat of Napoleon, the Congress of Vienna incorporated Illyria into Austria. Although parts of Croatia were governed by different branches of the Austro-Hungarian Empire, the eastern borders of Croatia and Bosnia-Hercegovina were well established by 1848. In the west, Istria, the city of Zadar and several Dalmatian islands would remain under Italian control until 1943.

Serbian Expansionism

Even when still an Ottoman principality, Serbia gained territory in 1833 and 1878, bringing its size to some 18,500 square miles. The newly established Serbian state began almost immediately to covet its neighbors lands and developed the official slogan "Serbia must expand or die!" Serbian expansionism was first directed toward the south into Macedonia and west toward the Adriatic through Bosnia and Hercegovina. In order to thwart Serbia's westward expansion, the Austrian protectorate of Bosnia-Hercegovina was annexed to the Empire in October 1908. As various European powers took sides supporting Austria-Hungary or Serbia in diplomatic and military alliances, the groundwork was laid for confrontation and the outbreak of the First World War.

Deprived of Bosnia, Serbia turned to Macedonia, then a part of the Ottoman Empire. The Balkan War of 1912 freed Macedonia from Turkey but led to a dispute over the spoils between the victors Bulgaria and Serbia. Aided by Greece and Romania, Serbia defeated Bulgaria and took the lion's share of Macedonia and all of Kosova. Only the establishment of a new Albanian state prevented Serbia from reaching the Adriatic.

Croatia Within the Habsburg Empire

When the Croatians elected a Habsburg as their king in 1527, they did so with the understanding that the crown would respect the rights, laws and customs of the Croatian Kingdom. While this principle was often violated by Hungary and Austria, Croatia maintained a great deal of autonomy and its ancient *Sabor* or Parliament and *Ban* or Viceroy. By 1914 the Croatians were on the verge of restoring their full political rights within the Empire.

The heir to the throne, Franz Ferdinand, was a liberal thinker who envisioned a new Empire based upon greater recognition of the Kingdom of Croatia. The Prince envisaged replacing the "Dualism" of Austria-Hungary with the "Trialism" of Austria-Hungary-Croatia or even a federal system based upon the American or Swiss model under a single benevolent Emperor. The thought of such a Croatian state, perhaps encompassing Bosnia-Hercegovina, presented a major threat to Serbia's dream of westward expansion and a "Greater Serbia." On June 28, 1914, Gavrilo Princep, a member of the Serbian terrorist group "Black Hand" assassinated Archduke Ferdinand and his wife in Sarajevo. Princep was one of seven assassins sent by Colonel Dragutin "Apis" Dimitrijević, Chief of Serbian Intelligence. Within weeks the world was at war.

Yugoslavia

Serbia made no secret of its ambitions in the War. As early as September 4, 1914 the Serbian government circulated a letter to all of its diplomatic missions calling the war an opportunity to create "a strong southwest-Slav state (to) be created out of Serbia, in which all Serbs, Croats, and Slovenes would be included." Serbia was more than willing to bargain away Croatian lands to Italy in a secret annex to the Treaty of London in 1915 in order to fulfill the dream of a Greater Serbia. Making use of the well intended but unelected Yugoslav Committee, Serbia with the backing of the victorious Allies, annexed Croatia, Bosnia-Hercegovina, Slovenia and Montenegro in 1918 into the new Kingdom of Serbs, Croats and Slovenes.

The borders of the Triune Kingdom of Croatia-Slavonia-Dalmatia and those of Bosnia-Hercegovina in 1918 were roughly those that had been in place since 1848. In the north Croatia gained two small territories from Hungary, Medimurje and Baranja, but lost several coastal islands to Italy in negotiations between 1918 and 1920.

When King Alexander declared himself absolute dictator and changed the name of the country to Yugoslavia in 1929 he abolished the traditional borders and reorganized the country into nine *banovinas* and the prefecture of Belgrade. Croatia was divided into the 15,649 square mile *Banovina* of Savska, primarily Croatia proper and Slavonia, and the 7,587 square mile *Banovina* of Primorska, primarily Dalmatia. While some traditionally Bosnian territory was added to Primorska *Banovina*, the oil and mineral rich region of Srijem, Croatian since 1718, went to the Serbian *Banovina* of Dunavska.

The *Banovina* of Croatia

From 1918 through 1938, Yugoslavia had thirty-five governments with a total of 656 ministers. Only twenty-six had been Croatians. The top-heavy Army had 161 generals. One, in charge of supply, was a Croatian. In the elections of December 1938 the Croatian Peasant Party and its leader Vladko Maček were defeated by a very close count of 1,364,524 to 1,643,783 for the royalist government. Given the fraud and terrorism common to all Yugoslav elections, it was obvious that the Peasant Party had won a stunning victory. Even government figures confirmed that over 650,000 Serbs had voted for Maček. Despite this the Stojadinović government refused to recognize the results or form a coalition government.

Faced with the threat of armed rebellion, Prince Paul sacked Stojadinović and replaced him with Dragiša Cvetković, a former mayor of Niš and a person open to negotiation concerning the "Croatian Question." The result was the *Sporazum* or Agreement of August 26, 1939 which formed the semi-autonomous *Banovina* of Croatia covering 38,600 square miles with a population of almost four and one-half million, 80 per cent of whom were Croatian. The new Croatian *Banovina* was connected to Yugoslavia only in matters of defense, foreign relations and a common postal system. Its borders included all of the two previous *Banovinas*, portions of western Bosnia and parts of western Hercegovina. Eastern Srijem and the strategic bay of Kotor with the southernmost tip of Dalmatia remained in Serbian hands.

The Independent State of Croatia

The formation of the Banovina of Croatia was a gesture that could have saved Yugoslavia in 1918, but coming only a week before the outbreak of World War II, it was simply too little, much too late. When Yugoslavia disintegrated at the first sign of German troops, a new Independent State of Croatia, known by its Croatian initials *NDH*, was founded on April 10, 1941. Its borders, which incorporated Bosnia-Hercegovina, were finalized by the Treaty of Rome on May 18. While Germany was willing to recognize the pre-1918 borders of Croatia and Bosnia-Hercegovina in the new state, Italy demanded and received most of the Dalmatian coast and set up an occupation zone comprising almost one third of the country. The *NDH* covered some 46,300 square miles with a population of 6,750,000. Internally the state was divided into 23 prefects or *velike župe* which were further divided into 142 districts and cities. Although Italian Dalmatia technically reverted back to the *NDH* upon the fall of Italy in 1943, much of the region was in Partisan control for the remainder of the War.

The Second Yugoslavia

Tens of thousands of Croatians fought and died in the 39 Croatian Partisan brigades that began the Liberation War under Josip Tito on June 22, 1941. The Partisans promised a new Croatian Republic, with full rights and autonomy, within a new federated Yugoslavia.

After the Partisan victory, a commission was established to set the borders of the new Yugoslav state. That commission was headed by Milovan Djilas, a Serb from Montenegro, and included ministers from Serbia, Croatia and Vojvodina. In the west, Croatia regained all of Italian Dalmatia, including Zadar and Istria. After years of negotiations the border was finalized in 1954 with Croatia gaining most of Istria, the city of Zadar and those islands occupied by Italy between the World Wars. In the south, the commission gave Montenegro access to the sea by removing the port of Kotor and the surrounding districts

CROATIA 1848-1918

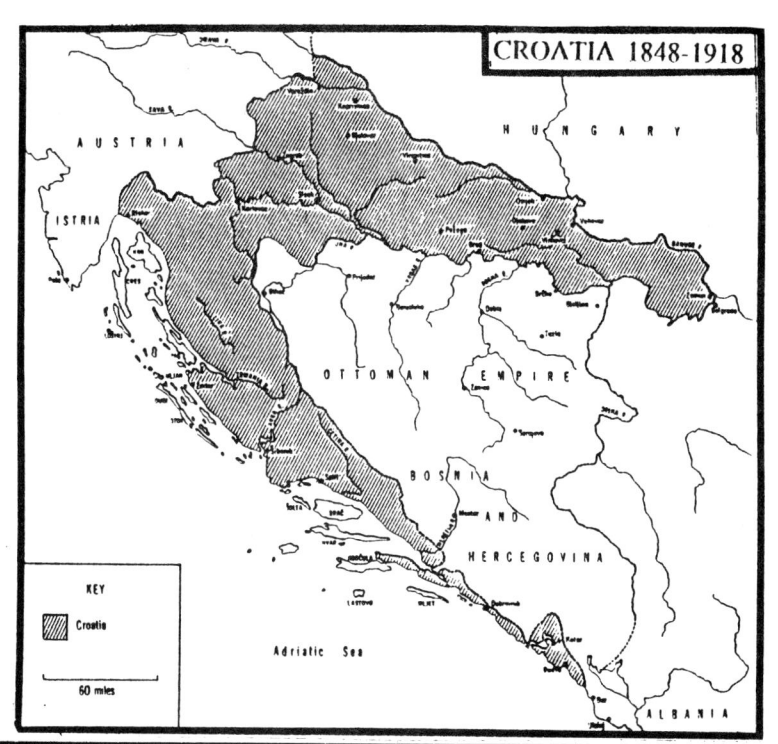

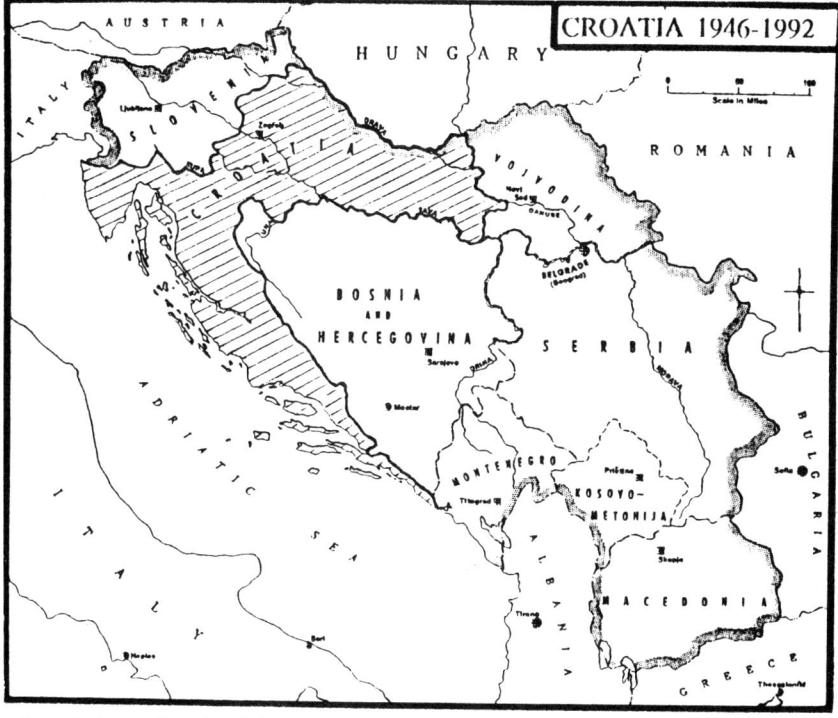

CROATIA 1946-1992

Croatia Land, People, Culture. 67

from Croatia. In the north Croatia's border returned to its pre-war configuration with the inclusion of Medjimurje and Baranja which had been Hungarian prior to 1918 and which had been seized by Hungary during World War II.

The borders of the Banovina of Croatia included a great deal of territory traditionally part of Bosnia-Hercegovina, including the cities of Travnik and Mostar. In 1945 the border was returned to 1918 boundaries with minor adjustments in the Bihac area where a number of Croatian villages were given to Bosnia-Hercegovina. But it was on the border with Serbia that Croatia would take its greatest territorial loss in 1945. The oil and mineral rich eastern Srijem region with the city of Zemun, Croatian territory since 1718, but partitioned by Alexander in 1929, was joined to Serbian Vojvodina.

The Republic of Croatia

The Croatian people again declared themselves to be free and independent on June 25, 1991. One year later, virtually the entire world had recognized Croatia within the borders designated in 1945. The overwhelming majority of Croatia's twelve hundred mile border is based upon ancient boundaries that Croatia brought with her into Yugoslavia in 1918. In those areas where the borders were changed, Serbia gained and Croatia lost. Despite this basic reality, the Republic of Croatia has made no territorial claims against any other nation; nor has Slovenia, Bosnia-Hercegovina or Macedonia. Serbia and Serbia alone since 1813 has constantly expanded in pursuit of the dream of a Greater Serbia stretching from Bulgaria to the Adriatic Sea. It is a dream that has cost the lives of millions over the past century and one-half and brought the worst fighting to Europe since World War II. How many more will die for Serbia's dreams of empire remains to be seen.

MYTH:
"SERBS HAVE NO RIGHTS IN CROATIA"

Myth: The government of the Republic of Croatia denied basic civil, cultural and linguistic rights to the Serbian minority in Croatia.

Reality: On the very day it declared independence Croatia granted extraordinary rights and privileges to Serbs and other minorities in Croatia.

It became apparent throughout the world that Serbia was the aggressor in Slovenia, Croatia and Bosnia-Hercegovina during the break-up of Yugoslavia. Its clear aim was the preservation of a Greater Serbian state while retaining the name Yugoslavia against the expressed will of the majority of the people. However, Serbia's aims were not so clear to many in the West during the terrible days of aggression in the Fall of 1991 and Spring of 1992.

A full-scale Serbian propaganda campaign repeated time and time again that the War was to "protect the Serbian minority in Croatia" despite the fact that the Serbs had lived peacefully with the Croatians for nearly a half-century. To reinforce their case, Serbia let it be known to the world that the new Croatian government had made no provision for the rights of Serbs in Croatia. The Western media, unable or unwilling to read the documents provided to them by the Croatian government in English, accepted mythology as fact and in many cases continued to repeat it well into 1992. "The Croatians wrote a new constitution, giving no special rights to Croatia's Serbs..." wrote the *Christian Science Monitor* on September 19, 1991.

Croatian Declaration of Independence, June 25, 1991

In reality, with the very first document to emerge from the new Croatian Republic, its Declaration of Independence on June 25, 1991, the Croatian government guaranteed not only civil rights, but unique rights to the Serbian minority. The first two articles of the Declaration established the rights of Croatia to declare independence and to defend its territorial integrity. Article III of the Declaration stated:

> The Republic of Croatia is a democratic, legal and social state in which prevails the supreme values of constitutional order: freedom, equality, ethnic equality, peace, social justice, respect for human rights, pluralism and the inviolability of personal property, environmental protection, the rule of law, and a multi-party system.
>
> The Republic of Croatia guarantees Serbs in Croatia and all national minorities who live in this territory the respect of all human and civil rights, especially the freedom to nurture their national language and culture as well as political organizations.
>
> The Republic of Croatia protects the rights and interests of its citizens without regard to their religious, ethnic or racial belonging.

In accordance with customary and positive international law, the Republic of Croatia guarantees other states and international bodies that it will completely and consciously uphold all its rights and duties as a legal successor to the previous Socialist Federal Republic of Yugoslavia to the extent that they relate to the Republic of Croatia.

In order to avoid bloodshed and insure a peaceful transition, the Croatian Declaration concluded:

The Republic of Croatia calls upon the other republics of the former SFRY to create an alliance of sovereign states on the presumptions of mutual recognition of state sovereignty and territorial integrity, mutual respect, recognition of political pluralism and democracy, pluralism of ownership and market economy, and the actual respect of human rights, rights for ethnic minorities and other civilized values of the free world.

Serbia met this call for peaceful dialogue with the bloodiest warfare Europe had seen since World War II, slaughtering over ten thousand people, exiling hundreds of thousands and crushing the human rights of non-Serbs in every corner of former Yugoslavia.

Charter Relating to the Rights of Serbs and Others

In order to dispel any doubts about the Croatian government's commitment to human rights and exceptional rights for the Serbian minority, the Croatian Parliament in its first session as an independent state, adopted *The Charter Relating to the Rights of Serbs and Other Nationalities in the Republic of Croatia* on June 25, 1991:

I. A just solution relating to the issue of Serbs and other nationalities in the Republic of Croatia is one of the important factors to democracy, stability, peace and economic advancement, and to cooperation with other countries.

II. The protection and full realization of rights for all nationalities in the Republic of Croatia, as well as the protection of individual rights is a composite part of international protection of human and civil rights and the protection of nationalities and as such they belong to the area of international cooperation.

III. The rights of nationalities and international cooperation will not allow any activity which is opposed to the regulations of international law, especially sovereignty, territorial integrity and the political independence of the Republic of Croatia as a united and indivisible democratic and social state.

IV. All nationalities in Croatia are legally protected from such activities that would threaten their existence. They have the right to respect and to self preservation of their cultural autonomy.

V. Serbs in Croatia and all nationalities have the right to proportionally engage in bodies of local self-government and appropriate government bodies, as well as security for economic and social development for the purpose of preserving their identity and for the protection of any attempts of assimilation, which will be regulated by law, territorial organization, local self-government as well as institutionalizing parliamentary bodies which will be responsible for relations between nationalities.

VI. Organizations which will adhere to the aims of its constitution and which are involved in protecting and developing individual nationalities, and as such are representative of the said nationality, have the right to represent the nationality as a whole and each individual belonging to that nationality, within the Republic as well as on an international level. Individual nationalities and members have the right, in order to protect their rights, to turn to international institutions which are involved in the protection of human and national rights.

The commitments of the Croatian government to human rights surpassed those of the United States Declaration of Independence which referred to native Americans as "merciless Indian savages," or the U.S. Constitution which specifically defined an African-American as three-fifths of a person.

The Croatian Parliament further strengthened the law on December 4, 1991 by specifically granting local police, courts and governments to Serbs in those areas in which they were a majority. These documents grant Serbs and other national minorities full protection of human rights, guaranteed proportional representation in government, the right to self-government, and protection from any attempts of forced assimilation. It further encouraged individuals and organizations to appeal to international bodies to secure these protections.

Ironically, Serbs in Croatia have never needed these provisions. It was the Croatians, Bosnians and Kosova's Albanian majority who would appeal to the European Community, the United Nations, the International League for Human Rights, Helsinki Watch, Amnesty International and other international bodies for protection from the Serbian minority and the Serbian controlled Army.

MYTH:
"TUDJMAN IS A RECENT CONVERT FROM COMMUNISM TO DEMOCRACY"

Myth: Until recently Croatian President Franjo Tudjman was a Communist Yugoslav Army general. Both Tudjman and Serbian President Slobodan Milošević are recent converts from Communism.

Reality: Dr. Franjo Tudjman resigned his Army commission in 1961. He has since been a strong advocate of democracy in Croatia and was imprisoned for his views. Slobodan Milosović simply changed the name of his party from Communist to Socialist before the 1990 elections.

Franjo Tudjman's long and difficult transition from Yugoslav Army general to President of the Republic of Croatia was as remarkable as the man himself. Franjo Tudjman was born on May 14, 1922 in Veliko Trgovišće in the Zagorje province of Croatia. At the age of nineteen, he joined the Partisans and became a decorated war hero.
  Like tens of thousands of Croatians who fought with the Partisans, he believed that a new federated Yugoslavia would guarantee the rights of the Croatian nation which had been trampled by the government of Royalist Yugoslavia. The Nazis put a price on Tudjman's head and killed his brother in 1943. Both of Tudjman's parents were killed by the Communists in 1946.

After the War, Tudjman was sent to the advanced military academy in Belgrade. His exceptional abilities led to his appointment as the youngest general in Yugoslavia. After twenty years of service, he left the army with the rank of major general in 1961 at age thirty-eight.

From 1961 through 1967, Tudjman was the Director of the Institute for the History of the Party in Croatia, linked to the Central Committee of the League of Communists. He was a respected member of the Party and held a number of senior political positions.

As director of the Institute, he devoted himself entirely to scholarly work and was appointed professor of History at the University of Zagreb in 1963. He obtained his doctorate two years later, specializing in the history of royalist Yugoslavia from 1918-1941. Although the government would not allow his dissertation to be published, his scholarship was such that he was appointed to the board of *Matica Hrvatska*, the Croatian Academy.

He published a number of works in the fields of military studies, history, philosophy and international relations. His 1981 book *Nationalism in Contemporary Europe* foretold the great European upheaval a full decade before the tumultuous events of 1991.

In 1965, Tudjman was elected to Parliament. At 43 years old, Franjo Tudjman was one of the most respected men in Yugoslavia: a retired major general, member of Parliament, Professor of History, Director of the Institute for the History of the Worker's Movement, Editor of the Yugoslav Military Encyclopedia and the Encyclopedia of Yugoslavia and a dozen other powerful positions in the Party, government and academic community. It was in that year that Secret Police Chief Aleksandar Ranković began planning for the 25th anniversary of the Liberation War to be observed in 1966.

A part of the celebrations would include dedication of a monument to the "700,000 to 900,000" people who died at the Jasenovac concentration camp. Tudjman, whose Institute had collected the actual number of war deaths in a secret report to be used in gaining war reparations from Germany, knew that Ranković's figures were inflated by at least ten fold. Tudjman was told not to make trouble for Ranković, Tito or the Party. Tudjman suggested that the data from his scholarship be made public. The data were later made public by Bruno Bušić, an associate of the Institute in 1969. Bušić was forced into exile where he was murdered by the Yugoslav Secret Police in 1978.

The Fall

Immediately, Tudjman's appointment to the Yugoslav Academy was voided and he was removed as Director of the Institute for the History of the Labor Movement by Ranković. Even Ranković's own fall in 1966 did not save Tudjman from mounting persecution. By 1967 he was removed from all offices and duties for stating his views on history and the Croatian language. In 1969, he lost his seat in Parliament. At the same time, Franjo Tudjman became one of the leaders of the great liberalization movement known as the Croatian Spring. That movement reached its peak in the Fall of 1971 before being ruthlessly crushed by Tito and his hardline Communist government in December of that year.

On October 12, 1972, after a brief so-called trial, Tudjman was sentenced to two years' imprisonment for counter-revolutionary activity and "hostile activity against the State." Upon appeal, the charges were changed to "hostile propaganda" and he was released after nine months and stripped of his civil rights including the right to publish, speak in public or travel outside the country. In 1977 Tudjman violated this ban by granting an interview to Swedish television. Although the interview was blocked by a diplomatic protest from Yugoslavia, Swedish television aired a one minute excerpt and the text was published in Sweden's *Dagens Nyheter* and Germany's *Der Spiegel* in October 1977. Within months it had been translated into English and published throughout the world. In 1979, Tudjman was named co-chairman of the International Democratic Committee to Aid Democratic Dissidents in Yugoslavia, a New York based human rights organization.

On November 17, 1980 Tudjman was again indicted for the crime of "maliciously and falsely representing socio-political conditions in Yugoslavia." The Communist's Orwellian doublespeak may have reached its apex when, in an indictment for speaking to a foreign reporter, the prosecutor wrote: "It is well known that (Tudjman's statements) are untrue because in the SFRY not only in its constitutional and legal decrees, but in the everyday life of its inhabitants as well, complete equality of all nations and nationalities in all areas has been realized, as has full freedom of the expression of opinion." Tudjman's eloquent defense was published in a number of languages and became a part of the literature for the democratization of Yugoslavia. "Everything I said was an expression of my personal belief in accordance with the ideals for which I fought in the Socialist Revolution and the anti-Fascist War" he said.

Despite any evidence against him, Tudjman was sentenced to three years in jail and loss of all civil rights for eight years. Before entering prison in November 1981, he was admitted to a Zagreb hospital with a heart condition. Despite a world-wide outcry that included the naming of Tudjman as a "Prisoner of Conscience" by Amnesty International, Tudjman was sent to the infamous Lepoglava prison in January 1982 where he suffered a series of four heart attacks. Another investigation was launched in 1988 in yet another attempt to silence Tudjman but by then the direction of the tide in Europe was clear. His civil rights were restored, he obtained a passport and undertook the foundation of a new political movement.

HDZ and Victory

On November 29, 1989 Tudjman and his newly formed Croatian Democratic Union, known by its Croatian initials *HDZ*, issued an appeal to the citizens of Croatia and to its Communist controlled Parliament to form a new multi-party government. The appeal called for a repeal of the Communist Party monopoly, secret and direct elections for Parliament, unrestricted travel for Croatian emigrants and freedom for political prisoners.

During this transition period the HDZ was the first internal party to expressly call for self-determination for Croatia, including the right to secession. Although the Yugoslav Constitution specifically guaranteed that right, to voice such a sentiment was considered treason by the Belgrade government.

In light of the dramatic changes sweeping Europe, the Croatian Parliament voted in February 1990 to legalize opposition parties and grant freedom of political affiliation. In April and May the first free elections in half a century were held in Croatia with some twenty political parties competing for seats in Parliament. Tudjman's Croatian Democratic Union won a landslide victory with 205 of 349 seats. The Communists who had ruled for a half century secured only 77 seats. Franjo Tudjman was elected President of the Republic.

On July 26, 1990 the Parliament dropped the word "Socialist" from the name Republic of Croatia and ordered the red star removed from all state symbols. Still, Tudjman and the Croatian government sought a new accommodation with the other republics of Yugoslavia through a confederation of sovereign states. Serbia's unwillingness to even negotiate for such a confederation led Croatia and Slovenia to declare independence on June 25, 1991 at which time Franjo Tudjman became the first President of the independent Republic of Croatia.

Slobo, "The Butcher of the Balkans"

Franjo Tudjman's long and arduous journey from Partisan war hero to president of his country was very unlike that of Serbian President Slobodan Milošević, whom the *New York Times* labeled the "Butcher of the Balkans." Milošević, an unrepentant hard-line Communist in the mold of Joseph Stalin, is a product of Communism and the Yugoslav Party-State.

Known to his few friends as "Slobo," he was born in 1941 in Pozarevac, near Belgrade, the son of a Serbian Orthodox priest from Montenegro and a hardline Communist school teacher. His father abandoned his family, taking Slobo's brother Bora with him. Both of his parents committed suicide and Milošević literally grew up in the Party. He married Mirjana Marković, a professor of Marxist theory who controlled the Communist League for Yugoslavia. She was a member of one of Yugoslavia's best known Communist families. Milošević lived such a secretive life at a villa on the outskirts of Belgrade that one of his closest friends admitted to a reporter from the *New York Times Magazine* that in twenty years he had never seen Milošević's home or his wife.

Under the mentorship of Ivan Stambolić, the previous Serbian Party boss, Milošević rose through the ranks from being director of the energy company *Tehnogas* to the Presidency of Belgrade's main bank. In the mid-1980's Stambolić elevated him to head of the Communist Party of Serbia. By way of thanks, Milošević engineered a *coup* within the Party in the fall of 1987, overthrowing his old friend and mentor Stambolić, and naming himself the undisputed head of Party and government in Serbia.

Milošević immediately set to work purging the leadership of Vojvodina, Kosova and the Republic of Montenegro to bring those constitutionally autonomous regions into line with his "Greater Serbia" policies. Many who opposed his policies, including Branislav Matić, a key opposition leader in the Serbian Renewal Movement, were murdered. Another SRM leader, George Božović, mysteriously fell from a high building.

As the rest of Europe was abandoning Marxist-Leninism, Milošević reinstated courses in Marxist theory in Serbia's schools and colleges. In January 1990 at the last Congress of the League of Communists of Yugoslavia, Milošević stormed the podium to declare that Communism would go on even without Slovenia and Croatia. But the realities of Europe in the 90's eventually came home to roost even for Milošević. In the Fall of 1990, he renamed the Communist Party the "Socialist Party" before winning 61% of the vote in the Party controlled "free" elections. Milošević's transformation from Stalinist to "democrat" was thus complete. In April 1992 he finally consented to the removal of the red star from Yugoslavia's flag.

History will judge which of the two men, Franjo Tudjman or Slobodan Milošević, fought for his country, suffered for his beliefs and liberated his nation and which unleashed a massive war of aggression against his neighbors to sustain Communism in Europe and the myth called Yugoslavia.

MYTH:
"THE CROATIAN COAT OF ARMS IS A FASCIST SYMBOL."

Myth: The Croatian twenty-five field "chessboard" coat-of-arms and the red, white and blue flag bearing that coat-of-arms are Fascist symbols.

Reality: The ancient Croatian coat-of-arms has been used for hundreds of years by every Croatian government, and was used by both royalist and Communist Yugoslavia.

The tale that the Croatian coat-of-arms is a symbol of Fascism is a very new myth that, like many others, was created by the Serbian apologist writers David Martin and Nora Beloff and has been repeated by some other ill informed reporters. "They waved the Croat checkered flag-something akin to waving a Confederate flag at an NAACP meeting" wrote the *Christian Science Monitor*. "Today again the Ustashe flag has been raised" cried Nora Beloff in the *Washington Post*. "Mr. Tudjman's decision to adopt a flag modeled on the Ustashe flag has only made matters worse," lamented David Martin writing in the *New York Times*.

It is ironic that those who repeat this myth do not mention or perhaps do not know that the government of Serbia from 1945 onward continued to use the same coat-of-arms used by the Nazi government of General Milan Nedić during World War II. The Serbian arms, which appeared so prominently on the world's most viciously anti-Semitic postage stamps during the War, continued to be proudly displayed by the Communist Serbian regime.

Hrvatski Grb

The *Hrvatski Grb* or Croatian shield is one of the oldest national symbols in Europe. The true origins of the *Grb* have been lost to antiquity. Croatian mythology once said that King Stjepan Držislav who ruled Croatia from 969 to 997 defeated a Venetian prince at chess to maintain Croatia's freedom. In fact Venice was defeated by Croatia in a sea battle in 887 and was forced to pay tribute to Croatia until 1000. There are many other myths regarding the origins and the exact design of the shield.

Many scholars believe that the Croatians originated in what became modern day Persia or Afghanistan where they were mentioned in the cuneiform inscriptions of the Persian King Darius the Great (522-486 B.C.E.). The design of the *Grb*, red and white alternating fields, may have been related to the ancient Persian system linking colors with direction which gave us such terms as the Red Sea and the Black Sea. The terms White Croatia and Red Croatia for western and southern Croatia were still in use well into the eleventh century. Silver seems to have been interchangeable with white throughout history.

The oldest known use of the *Grb* in Croatia is to be found on the wings of four falcons on a baptismal font donated by King Krešimir IV (1056-1073) to the Archbishop of Split. The *Grb* was used on document seals from the fifteenth century and can be found dating from 1490 in

CROATIAN COATS-OF-ARMS

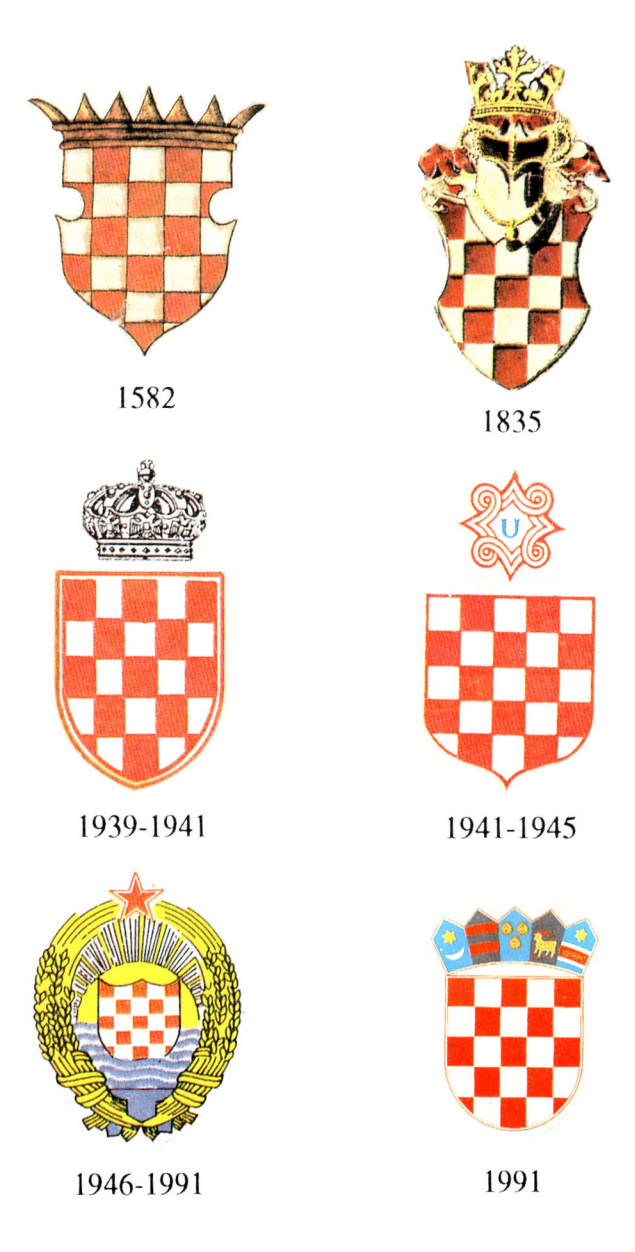

1582

1835

1939-1941

1941-1945

1946-1991

1991

the cathedral of Sinj and a church on the island of Krk.

Although the *Grb* is usually in its classic five-by-five form, there are numerous variations in history. One example is the charter of the Croatian Sabor or Parliament dated January 1, 1527 displays a shield of sixty-four fields. Perhaps best known to Croatians and tourists alike is the roof tile design of historic St. Mark's church in old Zagreb incorporating the coat-of-arms of the triune Croatian Kingdom and the City of Zagreb. St. Mark's was built in the thirteenth century and beautifully restored between 1876 and 1882.

Red or White?

Croatians have debated for generations whether the first of the twenty-five fields should be in white or red. Historically, red was more common for Croatia proper while white was more common in Bosnia. For most of Croatia's history both versions could be found. Prior to the revolution of 1848 red was most common. In 1848 the design was codified with twenty-five fields beginning with a white field. The *Grb* was incorporated into the state arms of the Austro-Hungarian Empire, as can be found on the beautiful coinage of Empress Maria Theresa.

When the Kingdom of Serbs, Croats and Slovenes which would become Yugoslavia was formed in 1918, the first field reverted to red. King Alexander Karageorgević ordered the Yugoslav coat-of-arms and his personal arms to incorporate the *Grb*, red field first. It is ironic that those who called the *Grb* an affront to all Serbs were unaware that it was superimposed on the Serbian double-headed eagle by the last Serbian King and remained there throughout the life of royalist Yugoslavia. Even in exile the Serbian would-be royalty continued to use the Croatian coat-of-arms as a part of their royal seal.

Following years of struggle for greater autonomy, Croatia became a semi-autonomous *Banovina* in 1939. The *Banovina* retained the *Grb*, red premier field and added a Crown above the shield. The *Ustaše* regime of World War II changed the first field to white and replaced the Royalist crown with a "U" for *Ustaše* above the shield.

When the Partisans emerged victorious in 1945 they introduced a Soviet-style coat-of-arms with the usual sheaves of grain surmounted by a red star. Prominently in the center of the shield was the ever-present twenty-five field *Grb* with the first field back to red. It was the Communists who first insisted that red and only red could be used. At one time it was a crime to display the *Grb* with a premier white field. Whether through error or intent, the last Constitution of the Socialist Federal Republic of Yugoslavia adopted in 1974 displayed the arms of Croatia with a white premier field!

In May 1990 when democracy was restored, tens of thousands of red, white and blue flags with the ancient *Hrvatski Grb* appeared from hiding places to replace the red star of Communism. The new Croatian government retained the traditional Croatian shield, red field first, with a five pointed crown representing the coats-of-arms of five of Croatia's historical regions.

The Croatian flag and the Croatian coat-of-arms were carried into battle against the Turks. They were carried into battle by Croatian-American GIs in World War I, and they were carried joyously through the streets of Croatia in 1990. The flag and coat-of-arms pre-date the arms of many European states and were in common use when Columbus set sail for India only to bump into America along the way. This is the proud reality of the *Hrvatski Grb*.

THE FINAL MYTH: "YUGOSLAVIA"

Croatians and Serbs lived side-by-side in peace until 1918. Croatia took in thousands of Serbian refugees from the advancing Turks and supported Serbia's bid for independence from the Ottoman Empire. It was only in 1918, when Serbia annexed Croatia as part of its newly expanded Kingdom that the hatred began.

The myth of Yugoslavia was reborn on November 29, 1945 when the Federal People's Republic of Yugoslavia was born as "a community of peoples who had freely expressed their will to remain united within Yugoslavia" despite the fact that no vote was ever taken. In 1990 and 1991 the peoples of Yugoslavia for the first time were allowed to vote for myth or reality. The peoples of Slovenia, Croatia, Bosnia-Hercegovina and Macedonia voted for reality in the form of freedom in a new Europe, an end to Communism and an end to multi-national empires. The peoples of Kosova and Vojvodina, enslaved in their own homelands, were given no vote.

On April 26, 1992 Serbian President Slobodan Milošević proudly announced the formation of a new Federation of Yugoslavia consisting of Serbia, Montenegro and the previously autonomous provinces of Vojvodina and Kosova. Like the two Yugoslavia's before it, this "state" was also a myth.

On August 2, 1992 over two and one-half million Croatians, representing seventy-five per cent of the electorate, again went to the polls in elections closely monitored by international observers headed by Lord Finsberg of the Council of Europe. In first-time direct elections for the Presidency, Franjo Tudjman received fifty-seven per cent of the vote in a race contested by eight major candidates. The second-place candidate received twenty-two per cent of the vote. The Croatian Democratic Union (HDZ) was returned to power in a Parliament reflecting a half-dozen political parties and all of Croatia's major ethnic groups. Croatia chose democracy.

Serbia chose Communism, expansion, war, and the continued myth of Yugoslavia. The Serbian leadership chose to launch an all-out war of aggression against her neighbors to force them to accept the Myth. When the entire free world finally recognized that Yugoslavia was indeed a myth, Serbia simply recreated it with the stroke of a pen backed by a few thousand tanks.

Some myths do not die an easy death.

BIBLIOGRAPHY

This monograph is intended to provide readers with the background of a few of the more common myths in a non-academic, readable format; therefore footnotes and endnotes were not used. However, dozens of articles and monographs have appeared covering many of the same myths over the years. The author wishes to acknowledge the work of every scholar, writer, and journalist who may have previously published articles about one or more of these legends. In addition to the authors of the books and chapters that follow, the author also wishes to specifically acknowledge the works of:

Alex Alexiev, Radoslav Artuković, Branimir Anzulović, Ljubo Boban, Bruno Bušić, Philip J. Cohen, Robert Guskind, Bogoljub Kočović, John Kraljić, Jakša Kušan, Branka Magas, Mirko Meheš, Petar Radielović, Hans Peter Rullmann, Carol J. Williams, and Vladimir Zerjavić.

BIBLIOGRAPHY

Books

Albrecht-Carrie, René. *Italy at the Paris Peace Conference*. Hamden, CT: Archon Books, 1966.

Beard, Charles A. and Radin, George. *The Balkan Pivot: Yugoslavia*. New York: Macmillan Company, 1929.

Beljo, Ante. *Genocide A Documented Analysis*. Translated by D. Sladojević-Šola. Sudbury, ONT: Northern Tribune Publishing, 1985.

Bilandžić, Dušan, *et al. Croatia Between War and Independence*. Zagreb: University of Zagreb, 1991.

Bonifačić, Antun and Mihanovich, Clement, Editors. *The Croatian Nation in its Struggle for Freedom and Independence*. Chicago: "Croatia" Cultural Publishing Center, 1955.

Croatia, Republic of. *Constitution of the Republic of Croatia*. Zagreb, 1991.

Croatia, Republic of. *Peace Conference on Yugoslavia: Croatian Approach*. Zagreb, 1991.

Dedijer, Valdimir; Božić, Ivan; Ćirković, Sima; Ekmečić, Milorad. *History of Yugoslavia*. New York: McGraw-Hill, 1974.

Epstein, Julius. *Operation Keelhaul*. Old Greenwich: Devin-Adair, 1973.

Eterovich, Adam. *Croatian and Dalmatian Coats of Arms*. Palo Alto, CA: Ragusan Press, 1978.

BIBLIOGRAPHY

Eterovich, Francis and Spalatin, Christopher, Editors. *Croatia Land, People, Culture.* 2 volumes. Toronto: University of Toronto Press, 1964 (I), 1970 (II).

Grakalić, Marijan. *Hrvatski Grb.* Zagreb: Nakladni Zavod Matice Hrvatske, 1990.

Grana, Gianni. *Malaparte.* Firenze: Il Castoro, 1968.

Hečimović, Joseph. *In Tito's Death Marches and Extermination Camps.* Translated and edited by John Prcela. New York: Carlton Press, 1962.

Hefer, Stjepan. *Croatian Struggle for Freedom and Statehood.* Translated by Andrija Ilić. Buenos Aires: Croatian Information Service, 1959.

Hoptner, Jacob. *Yugoslavia in Crisis 1934-1941.* New York: Columbia University Press, 1962.

Lederer, Ivo J. *Yugoslavia at the Paris Peace Conference.* New Haven: Yale University Press, 1963.

Letica, Slaven, Editor. *Croatia 1990.* Zagreb: Presidency of the Republic of Croatia, 1990.

Malaparte, Curzio. *Kaputt.* Translated by Cesare Foligno. New York: E. P. Dutton & Co., 1946.

Malaparte, Curzio. *The Skin.* Translated by David Moore. Malboro, VT: Marlboro Press, 1988.

McDonald, Gordon C., et al. *Area Handbook for Yugoslavia.* Washington: U.S. Government Printing Office, 1973.

BIBLIOGRAPHY

Milazzo, Matteo J. *The Chetnik Movement & The Yugoslav Resistance.* Baltimore: Johns Hopkins University Press, 1975.

Naval Intelligence Division. *Jugoslavia.* 2 vols. London: British Government, 1944.

Nikolić, Vinko. *Bleiburg Uzroci i Posljedice.* Munich: Knjižnica Hrvatske Revije, 1988.

Nyrop, Richard F., Editor. *Yugoslavia a country study.* Washington: Government Printing Office, 1982.

Omrčanin, Ivo. *The Pro-Allied Putsch in Croatia in 1944.* Philadelphia: Dorrance, 1975.

Prcela, John and Guldescu, Stanko, editors. *Operation Slaughterhouse.* Philadelphia: Dorrance, 1970.

Prpić, George J. *Croatia and The Croatians.* Scottsdale, AZ: Associated Publishers, 1982.

Ristić, Dragiša N. *Yugoslavia's Revolution of 1941.* University Park, PA: Penn State Press: 1966.

Roberts, Walter R. *Tito, Mihailović and the Allies 1941-1945.* New Brunswick: Rutgers University Press, 1973.

Singleton, Fred. *Twentieth-Century Yugoslavia.* New York: Columbia University Press, 1976.

Socialist Federal Republic of Yugoslavia. *The Constitution of the Socialist Federal Republic of Yugoslavia.* Translated by Marko Vavičić. Belgrade: 1974.

Stjepan Srkulj. *Hrvatska Povijest.* Zagreb: 1937.

BIBLIOGRAPHY

Tomasevich, Jozo. *The Chetniks*. Stanford: Stanford University Press, 1975.

Vrančić, Vjekoslav. *U Službi Domovine*. Buenos Aires, 1977.

Chapters in Books and Monographs

Babić, Ivan. "Military History." In *Croatia Land, People Culture, Vol I*. Edited by Francis H. Eterovich and C. Spalatin. Toronto: University of Toronto Press, 1964.

Benković, Theodore. *Tragedy of a Nation*. Chicago, 1946.

Cesarich, George W. "Yugoslavia was Created Against the Will of the Croatian People." In *The Croatian Nation*, pp. 192-211. Edited by Antun F. Bonifačić and Clement S. Mihanovich. Chicago: Croatian Cultural Publishing Center, 1955.

McAdams, C. Michael. *Allied Prisoners of War in Croatia 1941-1945*. Arcadia, CA: Croatian Information Service, 1980.

McAdams, C. Michael. *Whitepaper on Andrija Artuković*. Arcadia, CA: Croatian Information Service, 1975.

Tudjman, Franjo. *Croatia on Trial*. Translated by Zdenka Palić-Kušan. London: United Publishers, 1981.

THE AUTHOR

C. Michael McAdams is a specialist in Croatian studies and is Director of the University of San Francisco's Regional Center in the California state capital of Sacramento. Among his previous contributions to *CIS Monographs* were the *Whitepaper on Dr. Andrija Artuković* and *Allied Prisoners of War in Croatia 1941-1945*.

THE CROATIAN INFORMATION SERVICE

The Croatian Information Service was founded in 1974 as a non-profit news service and publishing house to provide information about Croatia and the Croatians to the world-wide journalistic, academic and political communities. CIS embraces the power of the written and spoken word as its sole methodology of change through the publication of magazines, bulletins, monographs, books and through the broadcast media. CIS is not affiliated with the government of the Republic of Croatia or any political party or organization in any country.

Análise Semiótica através das Letras